T0194987

SCIENCE
AND
FREE WILL

A Brief Introduction to
the Illusion of Free Will

SAM SHIPLEY

WESTBOW
PRESS®
A DIVISION OF THOMAS NELSON
& ZONDERVAN

WestBow Press books may be ordered through booksellers or by contacting:

WestBow Press
A Division of Thomas Nelson & Zondervan
1663 Liberty Drive
Bloomington, IN 47403
www.westbowpress.com
1 (866) 928-1240

ISBN: 978-1-9736-3754-7 (sc)
ISBN: 978-1-9736-3755-4 (hc)
ISBN: 978-1-9736-3753-0 (e)

Library of Congress Control Number: 2018910225

Print information available on the last page.

WestBow Press rev. date: 10/03/2018

DEDICATIONS

This book is dedicated to Daniel and Olivia Shipley, my two grandchildren who will forever remain dear to my heart. I pray that you will ask God for, and more importantly, use His protective shield of faith that you will need every minute of your lives.

PaPa

This book is also dedicated to other young Christians who will be introduced to the other side of free will, to the scars and wounds created from generations of a theological dispute over an issue that has arguably devoted more time than any other. Free will is an issue that, more than any other, represents the great divide between Calvinistic churches (known as Reformed) and the other many Christian churches which together, far outnumber the Reformed churches. Free will is the issue that separates these churches. As proof of the reliance on free will as a theological construct that separates these churches, you seldom hear the word "will" mentioned except in context with free will. Free will's entrenched status and dominance inform how far this giant will fall if ever brought down.

> "Our opinions are not in our own power; they are formed and governed much by circumstances that are often as inexplicable as they are irresistible."
>
> SPOKEN BY BENJAMIN FRANKLIN, WHO DID NOT EVEN KNOW HE WAS A CALVINIST AT HEART AND PROBABLY NOT A CHRISTIAN.

CONTENTS

BENEFITS OF A FETTERED WILL

The heroes of the reformed movement opened the doors of Calvinism, starting with Augustine, but the majority of Christendom ignored the clarion calls for bondage (fettering) from Luther and others. Bondage is just not vogue or democratic for the majority of Christians, who think God's sovereignty must be democratic enough for every believer to have equal say in the individual's salvation. Equal opportunity is emblazoned on every human rights law and chiseled on government buildings, but it's not treated as such in the Bible. God chose the Hebrews, who became a Jewish nation, without consulting them. God's choices throughout the Bible are too numerous to cite but include God's corporate choosing of the Hebrews and did not end with His chosen nation of Israel but extended to the analogous countless grains of sand of Abraham's offspring. Later, God's gathering of individual gentiles completed His choosing. Framing this into human's timeframe is misleading because the Bible tells us He made His choices "before the foundation." Everyone, including non-Christians, has a captive will, even those who believe in free will. Only three possible sources are claimed to control our wills: God, Satan (sin), and self, as believed by the freewill believer. But God is the only valid source due to His sovereignty. Nowhere in the Bible is there a suggestion that His choosing or electing involves freewill choices. Accepting that a Christian's will is captive (Paul also calls it "bondage") enables us to avoid the what-if syndrome.

I'm convinced we all experience this bothersome and sometimes toxic way of thinking. In my experience, before I learned that cause and effect was the operative marandi employed by God in His design of the universe, as well as being copied in His creation of us, I kept beating myself on the head for things I did wrong in addition to spending a lot of time in wishful thinking. Before I learned God's sovereignty entails individual and corporate choosing regarding salvation and events, I was distraught that some of my so-called freewill choices after my salvation were wrong. Some people use the term "determinism" as a synonym for sovereignty. Why was I spending remorseful time wishing I had made the seemingly fateful choice of not investing in Walmart stock in the 1960s? If I had, I would be a multimillionaire. This was just one of the hundreds of things I thought I could have done differently in a seventy-year period of my life.

Since understanding the difference between my conscious and unconscious minds, the forces of genetic disposition, and the pull of environmental causation, I am now free indeed. I thought I was free during the years I believed in free will. But I can now focus on details I never saw. I can see why God created us from dirt. He wanted our composition to be composed of dirt because He wanted it to be composed of carbon, hydrogen,

> *Age always outruns wisdom.*
> AUTHOR UNKNOWN

and so on, the same elements that comprise the universe. He wanted us to realize everything has a purpose and a rule of law, and nothing escapes His notice or preview. He wanted us to realize everything has the same rule, His rule. I believe I rightly corelate this to my nonmillionaire status and the hundreds of other things that hindsight's deception attempted to tell me could have happened. The universe will spawn dark holes. So be it. It will also spawn beautiful sunsets. My life will reflect the same scenarios displayed in nature—the dark times and the good times. Dark times in my life, and well as in the universe, are not as dark as we portray them. When we keep our eyes on Jesus, the Bible says that "all things work to the good to those who love God," (Romans 8:28) and that "the end of a thing is better than its beginning" (Eccl 7:8). If God pays attention to sparrows that fall, I extrapolate this to claim He is concerned more about me than a sparrow. Extrapolation is not needed to prove He is in control of everything that happens to me.

Many people believe I have overextended the boundaries of

sovereignty. All freewill narratives and some Reformed ones claim that if Calvinism's interpretation of sovereignty is correct, it would make responsibility and accountability for our actions mute and void. If God determines everything, they say, we should sit in our favorite rocker and let Him do all the work. This is reasonable, they say, because if He plans, ordains, and causes everything, He—not us—is responsible for our sins. But the Bible shows that the first Adam was (and is) responsible, and the Second Adam accepted that responsible at the cross. Sovereignty is far too weighty an issue to be addressed in a few paragraphs, and I defer to one of my favorite authors, Loraine Boettner, in his *The Reformed Doctrine of Predestination*, who uses eighteen scriptures and says, "Nothing can come to pass apart from His sovereign will."

Responsibility and accountability cannot be ignored. Just because God causes everything does not mean we are not accountable. There are two aspects to His sovereignty: His permissive will and His absolute will. If I get shot, it will be impossible to know which will is involved, even if law enforcement proves its homicide. This is because it's impossible for us to know if God allows or causes wars, earthquakes, floods, and so on. In some cases, we can know if it's His permissive will or absolute. We know He allowed a thorn in Paul's side, and this was absolute, expressly for the purpose of showing His abiding grace. I trust in the reason God did not make me wealthy.

My analogy in understanding why we are accountable is to use a mother's minute-by-minute care of a rowdy child. She may have caused her child to be spoiled, but should she let him throw food and scream? Good moms hold their children responsible by teaching them right from wrong, even though all kids are born rebellious. Should we hold them responsible for their sin nature? Yes. I am not saying God causes us to do bad things. Regardless of the cause, we are responsible. Jesus told the adulteress woman to go and sin no more, but she continued to sin. Even though she was forgiven her sins, she, like us, are accountable to the laws

> *"And you will know the truth, and the truth will make you free"* John 8:32

of the universe and our behaviors. We don't know 95 percent of the time why we do things, but we are still accountable.

If you believe in free will, you believe God's sovereignty is not all inclusive, that humankind's depravity is not total, that your salvation depends on something other than unconditional grace, that Christ's atonement was universal, that salvation for the elect is resistible, and that your election is not retroactive. You could benefit from this book by taking a closer look at how recent scientific discoveries have unraveled the fake news that have for centuries held free will together. Even if you believe in all or some of the above, you could still benefit from the realization that our conscious minds are not guardian agents of our behavior. Actually, this secular and scientific aspect is the hardest thing for people to accept, harder than believing that the only free will a Christian has is found in Christ and not in self. This book provides a direct link between scientific discovery regarding mind/brain behavior and the Bible, joining the two in a cohesive union that allows for objective analysis.

If I were a preacher, I would be using this book to preach by pointing out the link between science and the blood of Jesus. I would join science with the Bible without injury to the principle of *Sola Scriptura*. Since everything points to the cross, it needs to be pointed out that the Holy Spirit is the causative agent who can control the Christian's subconscious. While this book emphasizes the pitiful throes of our captivity to our unconscious minds, attention must be given to the divine guiding power of the Spirit. When we are not walking in the Spirit, and it's a Bible fact that we all spend too much time in our self-absorbed pursuit of "mind consciousness", this is the only way He can teach us. If I were a preacher, I would show that even if you believe in free will, God's saving grace overrides everything. Instead of emphasizing that we only consciously remember 5 percent of everything we ever did or will do, emphasis would be placed on keeping our declining memories from becoming the problem they are. We were born to physically and mentally decline as well as die but there are things that we can do to shore up our physical and spiritual well-being. We need to better deal with dementia. I know the heartache of seeing our loved ones who don't see us. We need to realize more emphatically that God is in control and take to heart the

Bible teaching that God will not allow any harm to come to our souls, yet accept the inevitable decline of aging. We need to keep in mind the difference between "harm" and "suffering." As shown in the book of Job, He will allow suffering and, as stated in other places, will not test us beyond what we can endure.

> "For God so loved the world, that he gave His only begotten Son, that whosoever believed in Him should not perish, but have everlasting life." (John 3:16)

INTRODUCTION

The veteran Christian, who is a believer in FW (free will) whose vociferous opposition to bondage of the will, is given scientific proof of the invalidity of free will. If the person disagrees with this proof or claims it to be irrelevant, he or she will be disagreeing with a mountain of supporting research that denies the validity of FW. This book contains only a few of the many projects completed since science finished gene mapping, thus marking the scientific death knell of FW. However, this funeral is ignored by the majority of the Christian FW-believing world. There are other books regarding mind/conscious functions and behavior caused solely by the unconscious mind or by influences outside the control of the chooser. These books have made an impact in dismantling the credibility of FW in the secular community. But the books I have read are laboriously laden with hard-to-understand scientific terms. I have attempted to make this book user friendly and dedicate it to the above readers. My most significant contribution is combining scientific discoveries with biblical issues, thus making bondage of the will understandable in both the secular and biblical realms. To my knowledge, no book or narrative has made compelling use of the principle of cause and effect in refuting FW.

I am not a scholar or theologian in the professional sense of the word because I have not relied on writing for income. However, I have studied and researched Calvinism for forty years and agree with many scholars, both Calvinists and free will teachers, who take the position that John Calvin's *Institutes of the Christian Religion* is so comprehensive that it encompasses the full scope of theology. I am taking this opportunity to be scholarly incorrect and speak to you from my heart in a personal manner as opposed to scholars who are prone to speak from the head and who wear the scholarly mantle required in scholarly works. I am referring to the scholarly rule that prohibits personal pronouns and a minimal use of personal experiences. The Calvinistic scholars I have read think a FW believer is unsaved. They base this on the FWers lack of acknowledging God's sovereignty. However, many Christians, both Calvinists and FW believers, do not give due credit to sovereignty but this is not grounds for labeling those believers as unsaved. I think the idea of sovereignty is misunderstood by many Christians, Calvinistic theologians included, and this misunderstanding can be likened to many other theological issues that separate Christian denominations. Some Christians think their salvation can be lost. Thinking this does not make them lost but what matters is can they be saved? Some think they can say no to God regarding salvation but what matters is can they say yes? Some think Man is not totally depraved before salvation but what really matters is if they believe they are depraved enough to need Christ's saving atonement. I believe the above people can be Christians but if they believe in FW it will not cost them their salvation but the cost will be a loss of blessings. All Christians believe that God dispenses blessings in a discretionary manner so there is not much disagreement when I claim that God gives more blessings to some than others. Most believe that our crowns in Heaven

> "You must learn to let go. Release the stress. You were never in control any way."
> STEVE MARABOLI

are based on good works. There are twenty-seven topical scriptures that deal with blessings and all are related to ways to receive them. If you believe in FW, you believe that you can reject God. Since this is not a good thing, you don't believe Romans 8:28. "And we know that God causes all things to work together for good to those who love God, to those who are called according to His purpose." How can a FWer have as deep a fellowship with God if he believes that he can reject God and loose that fellowship? To me, this is unnerving to know that my fellowship (or salvation) with God can be compromised by my wavering belief in my eternal security. Calvinists are known for their emphasis on eternal security. (Once saved always saved) Before becoming a Calvinist, I spent too much time worrying about things that are in God's domain. Calvinists are known and faulted for their interpretation of sovereignty but rightly believe that a side effect of Calvinistic sovereignty produces the feeling of security that surpasses all understanding.

The purpose of this book is not an attempt to discredit the fact that we are able to do and think and make decisions but to discredit the belief that we are consciously aware, most of the time, of what causes us to do and think and decide. Science has proven that our awareness is not what we think it is. This book can serve as an introduction to Calvinism but will also be useful to those who are well steeped in Calvinism and Free Will (FW) because it contains topics that I have never seen in the many Calvinistic narratives and books I have read. People who believe in FW are formally known as Armenians, named after James Arminius who inadvertently wrote an anti-Calvinist thesis that his followers turned into an attack on Calvinism which was later used as a FW document representing FW theology. I taught science in the public-school system and this is when I began to see the correlation between the cause and effect of physics and its impact on religion. Physics and many natural and life sciences contribute to a better understanding of the Bible and God. The naysayers who believe the two cannot mix are wrong when they say the role of science is to prove things we can see, feel, and hear and the role of religion is to prove, by faith, those things we cannot see, feel, or hear.

Science's time in the sun has now come even though both FWers and Calvinists are staying in the dark. I include Calvinists because its theologians have not gotten around to using the recent scientific discoveries that dispel FW. Theology has changed but in no way does this equal the sea change in science. We have gone past looking into the vast expanses of the galaxies and are now making headway in the mysterious

> *"A prayer a day keeps the spirit alive. An apple a day keeps the body alive."*

recesses of the mind and brain. Although exaggerated we are now trying to look into the mind of God Himself, i.e., The God Gene. Genesis 3:22

gives us a preview of what could have happened after the Fall by stating "Then the Lord God said, "Behold the man has become like One of Us, knowing good and evil, and now, lest he stretch out his hand, and take also from the tree of life, and eat, and live forever." This scripture denies the existence of FW after the Adamic post-fall and also gives us a hint of how powerful the Tree of Life is, which is the source of eternal life. This informs me that we could, if God permits, shatter the frontiers of the outer space of the universe as well as the inner space of the mind. Just recently, science has taken us past using wi-fi in our homes, which we no longer think of as unusual, to the unusual use of inductive (wireless) electrical transmission for recharging automobile batteries. Another notable invention is in the field of artificial limb technology in which a hand or foot can be made to move telegraphically, that is, a user can make his hand move by "thinking" his hand to move. These discoveries herald the advances in science as well as modern day insights in the mysteries of the mind. Cause and effect, the Bible, and science inform each other and their universal compatibility is proven by the universal laws of God. Advances in science are commensurate with continued proof of the invalidity of FW. Every action taken by man can be *explained* by the principle of cause and effect, leaving the principle of FW unable to *explain* anything.

A brief explanation is needed regarding "once saved always saved". This theology is shared by Calvinism and many denominations who share some of the Calvinistic tenets. The preservation of our salvation is anchored by many scriptures. Christ said no one can take His sheep from Him. Can this be construed in any possible interpretation as meaning His sheep can bolt the pen even though the gate has been eternally closed? FW, where has your power gone? Spiritual perpetuation can be divided into two realms, God's Kingdom where the saved will be secure forever, and Satan's domain, where the lost will be dammed. Calvinism teaches that the saved are God perpetuated. FW teaches that the saved are self-perpetuated by exercising the power to accept or reject salvation. A secular and biological aspect of perpetuation is genetic predisposition and is represented by some who believe that we are wired to believe in a higher authority, not necessarily wired to be saved. Calvinists and Reformers carry this a step further by believing that we are wired to be chosen "before the foundation." Biological perpetuation is merely a genetic function that, together with the environment, determines our earthly longevity. If FW was biblically valid, God's earthly and heavenly kingdoms would have two doors, one to go in when he chooses and one to go out when he chooses. Of the FW books I have read, I have not seen a plausible explanation that biblically explains how it is possible to lose one's salvation. The Bible teaches there is only one entrance door, Jesus, and no exit. When we become a Christian, this is our earthly ticket into the Heavenly Kingdom, meaning we do not have to wait until Jesus' second coming. It's strange to me that a FW believer believes that he can exchange his earthly ticket for one to Hell when he is living but agrees that once he is in Heaven, he is there to stay, no backing out. In the Christian community, there is probably only three doctrines that attempt to explain salvation, FW, salvation by works, and Calvinism.

An Introduction is needed to address some of the perceived negatives of Calvinism. It was named Calvinism by his followers. I do not believe he would have wanted a denomination, church, or theology named after him. He was not the first to bring a Calvinistic type of theology into the Church. Calvin died in 1565. In 387 A.D. Augustine was a Bishop in the Roman Catholic Church. His teachings on predestination were a forerunner to the later teachings of Calvinism and came twelve centuries before Calvin's five-point theology, which is known by its acronym TULIP. (total depravity, unconditional election, limited atonement, irresistible grace, and preservation of the Saints, the latter also known as once saved, always saved.) Augustine's teachings went against the grain of the Church but because he was so popular, the Church leadership condoned this teaching and never publicly denounced him or his teaching. What was extremely remarkable was he escaped the punishment of death because it was common in those days for anyone who taught anything contrary to Church dogma be put to death. Augustine was considered a heretic by many of the Church Elders who were jealous of his popularity.

For many years I have asked God questions that seem to have not been answered. I address this issue because it is a universal problem for everyone. My disappointment regarding these seemingly unanswered questions had prevented me from enjoying the full benefit of His blessings. Why didn't I make enough money so I could be happy? I tithed and prayed. Why did I contract the gene that caused my type one diabetes? Many good books have answered these types of questions. 2 Corinthians 12:9 in the Amplified Bible states "My grace is sufficient for you... and is completed and shows itself more effectively in your weakness." I, along with others, have abused this scripture by an attempt at humor in asking, "Well, maybe I should pray for a heart condition so that I can be more "completed." It goes on to say"...therefore, I will

> *"Consciousness explains things that have already been decided for you."*
> TERRY SEJNOWSKI
> DIRECTOR OF SALK'S COMPUTATIONAL NEUROBIOLOGY LABORATORY

all the more gladly boast in my weaknesses, so that the power of Christ may dwell in me." Paul wanted God to remove the thorn from his flesh. Verse 10 goes on to say "for when I am weak, then I am strong." No better fighting words than these that tell us how to overcome. This profound truth answers all our questions that seem to go unanswered. I asked God about my finances because I wanted the money for my self-aggrandizement, not because of Paul's goal that "the power of Christ may dwell in me." The above verses answer all those questions about world hunger, wars, evil, disease, martial failures, and any other humanitarian questions we could ask. However, there is still one huge question to be answered. If there were no bad things, no thorns in our sides, meaning if there was no sin, would we need the power of Christ in us? If none of those bad things existed and we had no weaknesses, we would have Heaven on Earth. But the only environment that can exist in the absence of sin is Heaven. The purpose of His power exists to elevate us from our weaknesses, "and is completed and shows itself more effectively in your weaknesses." The only answer is we were born into sin, and that of our own choosing, and therefore the need to have the power of Christ in us was caused by our choosing to die when Adam chose to die. In addition, as born-again sinners, God did not design us to be immune from disasters and heartache. I must be satisfied with this answer and not be concerned with the hypothetical question of what if there was no sin or why God did not make the world square.

Thus far in this book there is nothing unique that can't be read in many good books. It becomes unique when correlating this material with the issues of cause and effect and of bondage of the will (Calvinism). The only way we can have the power of Christ dwelling in us is having His will, not FW, in us and being bound by His will. A Christian who thinks he has his own FW actually has God's FW and is seeing a reflection of God in Christ, who is in every Christian regardless of theological belief. Being bound by His will doesn't mean that we no longer have a will. It means that, in regards to His chosen, we don't have the ability to "will", to choose Hell even if we think we do. His will can't live in harmony with FW but His long suffering allows it the same as He allows me to yell at someone who cuts me off on the highway. Mark 3:15 states "If a house is divided against itself, that house will not be able to stand." Having the power of Christ in us is having the ability to allow Christ's will to turn our weakness, our thorns and sins, into strength. Romans 8:28 states "And we know that God causes all things to work together for good to those who love God, to those who are called according to His purpose." How can we believe this scripture yet believe that everything coming from FW is good even though FW is untouchable by God? All good things come from God. The above "His purpose" is translated as His will. I have mentioned dozens of times in this book about what FW believers believe. If you doubt that they don't believe that their FW supersedes God's, just pick up any FW narrative.

The reason Paul did not itemize the sins he committed, nor did the other Apostles, is because we are not defined by the number of sins we commit. The Bible teaches that if we sin once, we are a total sinner yet can be saved and become as white as snow and our sins are forgiven. FW teaches that salvation can be lost numerous times, thus defining salvation as contingent on the number of times it takes to regain it, thus requiring Christ to die

> "We are not human beings having a spiritual experience. We are spiritual beings having a human experience."
>
> PIERRE TEILHARD DE CHARDIN

numerous times. If I am a Christian on Monday and lose it on Tuesday, my snow is melted and I wear a sin stained garment. I am a lost sinner again and if a Christian can lose his salvation, Christ has to die again. Thus, a FW believer is defined by the number of sins he commits, in effect by the number of times he decides to lose his salvation. Calvinism teaches that before salvation, we are totally depraved and a total sinner and after salvation, totally and eternally saved. One salvation is sufficient. FW teaches that we are partially depraved before salvation and after salvation, partially saved, depending on how many times we decide to lose our salvation. Calvinism teaches we are endowed with the inalienable right to be forever free from the penalty of death, from the bondage of Satan, and free to be voluntary bond servants to Christ, thus allowing Christ to indwell in us. Indwelling has the connation of living in and thus supplanting His will over ours in regard to our salvation.

Calvin, a French lawyer who is counted as one of the great theologians of his time, died in 1565 and left the legacy of his greatest work, *The Institutes of The Christian Religion*, as his literary Magnum Opus, which was one of the greatest religious works of his generation, a commendation given by even some non-Calvinists. (The King James Bible was completed in 1611). The "*Institutes ...*" was written during the cultural movement known as the Renaissance Period which occurred during the fourteenth to seventeenth centuries. This period followed the Medieval Period which occurred during the fifth to thirteenth centuries, which was known for its scholastic achievements. The "*Institutes ...*" is admired in modern times by many theologians who do not even believe in the tenets of Calvinism or agree with its conclusions but agree that it stands as one of the greatest systematic studies of the Bible because of its methodology. Calvin's advice to all newcomers who are just starting their learning of theology is: Do not begin this journey unless you plan on finishing it. It's best to not even start it if you don't finish. To stop before finishing will leave you with more questions than when you started and will leave you with a wrong understanding of

> "Sir, my concern is not whether God is on our side. My great concern is to be on God's side."
> ABRAHAM LINCOLN

his teachings. This advice was from a man who is credited with being the founder of one of the three great churches in Europe. I did not take Calvin's advice when I started my study of his *Institutes of the Christian Religion*. I refused to accept his, the Apostle Paul's, and Martin Luther's teachings of bondage of the will and predestination. Dependence on my Southern Baptist background would not allow me to give up my free will (FW). I gave up Calvinism when it could not tell me explicitly in terms I could understand why God chose some to be saved and not others. But Romans 9:16 states "So then it does not depend on the man who wills or the man who runs, but on God who has mercy." So, this denotes mercy as the reason for God's choosing but I wanted to know why His mercy was limited to His elect. At that point in my life, I wanted more than mercy as the reason. Although that was the reason Paul gave, I wanted more from Calvinism. But for a long time I continued to study and finally accepted that God chooses some and except for the reason of mercy, does not give us many details and owes us no explanation. We would not understand the reasons even if He told us. Many Christians ask God why he didn't spare the infants and children when He destroyed everyone in the world (or at least in the Middle East), except Noah's eight-member family. All God told us was the world had become evil. Not much detail here and until the last chapter of Job, he did not understand what God was doing or why. Non-Calvinists think they have the reason (in addition to mercy) why God chooses some but not others. It's simply if they first choose God, He chooses them.

You can't identify me as a Christian by looking at my fruit. Non-Christians produce good fruit and appear to have good faith but this is deceiving. James 2:18 tells us a Christian must have both faith and works (fruit). The Bible is clear in its proof that each of us can know if we are saved and an assurance of salvation is personal and is available to us individually but we cannot know for sure if someone else is a Christian by looking at his fruit or even hearing his testimony. As Christians, God wants us to be a part, even helper, in His salvation plan. He does the choosing and saving. We are the onlooking helpers. He may have chosen you to teach or preach to His chosen before they are saved and be His instrument in their salvation in order for you to receive rewards both on earth and in Heaven. Revelations 14:13 tells us "Write, Blessed are the dead which die in the Lord from henceforth; yea, saith the Spirit, that they may rest from their labors; and their works do follow them." I believe God uses both cheerleaders and preachers. My definition of being a Christian instrument is one of many who gather on the sidelines of God's great game of salvation who are waving and shouting for the unsaved chosen to run a good race, as Paul describes it, and reach the finish line. Having an assurance of one's salvation and identifying others who are saved are two difference things. The gospel must be preached to all. Paul's definition of "good race" is obvious. Each Christian is going to run his unique race. The mansions that God has provided for us are custom built and each one will have its own architecture which I believe are rewards for good works. Paul's definition of a good race is good works. We must understand the chronological order of salvation. Ephesians 1:4 tells us "just as He chose us in Him before the foundation of the world, that we would be holy and blameless before Him....." God chooses and we can't be saved until He redeems us. Just because He chose you does not mean that I don't need to be encouraging you from the sideline. In between the time of being chosen and saved, God has assigned preachers and helpers to be sideline cheerleaders. However, no one outside the reformed doctrine will agree that preachers and helpers are merely cheerleaders in a game that has already been won. Many unsaved people believe in FW and thus think it's their FW that saves them. A chosen person, either before salvation or after, can believe in FW because its perversion has no limits or boundaries. Just because someone believes he has FW does not mean he has it. The reason God permits a belief in FW is the same reason He permits a belief in Catholicism, Baptists, Church of Christ, Methodist, and the many other Jesus believing churches. The saving power of Jesus is not diminished by a belief in FW, even though the power of Jesus and FW are direct opposites. FW, if it existed, would be arbitrary and unstable and would change depending on circumstances. The power of Jesus never changes.

> "He who knows not and knows not that he knows not is a fool."
>
> ASIAN PROVERB

PREAMBLE

The principle of cause and effect has been available to the modern church but is regrettably seldom used to defend Calvinism. The biblical principle of Sola Scriptura (defined as "The Bible Only as Authority") was the only cogent theological argument accepted by the reformed churches beginning with the Protestant Reformation which was spearheaded by Martin Luther in the sixteenth century and adhered to by many denominations today. (What many modern-day Lutherans don't know is Luther was a hard-core Calvinist yet the Lutheran Church doctrine is not Calvinistic and believe in FW alongside the other Protestant churches). The words "science" and "scientist" were not invented until the early eighteen hundreds but now Christian scientists are beginning to have their voices heard in theological matters. For example, scientists have discovered the so-called God Gene, a gene that is thought to enable us to recognize the existence of a transcendental being higher than humans. The awesome breakthrough of gene mapping has indicated that animals do not have this gene. It seems to me that the religious community is beginning to accept science as a secondary authority as long as it is understood that the Bible is the primary authority and as long as science does not interfere with the institution of FW, but it does interfere in a head on confrontation and is ignored in favor of FW. In the fifteen hundreds, Luther's *Bondage of The Will* (anti FW) gained a strong foothold during the rise of the Protestant Reformation and bondage of the will was taught in many churches throughout Europe. For that matter, bondage was taught in the Puritan churches in the American colonies. It's ironic that in modern times, the doctrine of FW has gained a foothold at the same time that science is proving FWs folly. Luther's religious bondage doctrine, which is Calvinism, is supported by both secular science and the Bible yet is ignored by the majority of mainstream Christianity. Regardless of scientific proof that dispels the religious doctrine of FW, the majority of Protestant Churches teach FW and we are again back in the Dark Ages prior to Calvin, Luther and the Reformation. It must be pointed out that the central theme of Luther's doctrine, as stated in his book, was to teach that unsaved sinners cannot possibly have the FW ability to choose God since they are dead in their sins and spiritually dead men cannot choose and don't want to choose. Luther taught that God is the Chooser and Man *then* has the ability to choose God. Luther drives his knife further into the heart of FW by adding that when God chooses (as taught by Calvinists), the chosen can't refuse God's calling. FWers cannot mix this undemocratic element with religion because they believe our God's government is a democracy in which everyone has an equal right to vote himself into or out of the great salvation election. This democratic notion sounds good because it attempts to tie salvation to our democratic American way of life and the equal clause in our Constitution but it is not supported by the Bible. As God asked Job, "Where were you when I laid the foundation of the earth? ... ." (Job 38:4) This attempt to "democratize" a biblical doctrine subverts God's sovereignty by attempting to replace His will with man's. A reasonable interpretation of Genesis tells me that Adam had FW and ate from the Tree and thus he and all posterity lost it.

The lesson to be learned in the pre-Fall Garden was that FW was a two-edged sword, enabling Adam to obey and live forever or disobey and die. God told Adam he would die if he ate. Spiritually dead men can't have FW!!! 1 Corinthians 15:22 tells us "For as in Adam all die, so also in Christ all will be made alive". It must be pointed out that only those in Christ will be made alive. The Bible is clear that we are all dead at birth. How can FW make us alive at birth or

"I promise you nothing is as chaotic as it seems. Nothing is worth diminishing your health. Nothing is worth poisoning yourself into stress, anxiety, and fear."
STEVE MARABOLI

any other time? Adam, in his FW heyday, was spiritually alive at birth. This is the reason FW cannot exist again in its original format. God's design was to have one FW (pre-Fall), one Garden, one first Adam, (us) and one Second Adam, Jesus. Had He allowed FW to continue after the Fall, He would have permitted a replay which would have butted heads with the Cross and Christ would have had to die a second time for a second Adam. The Bible teaches that Jesus died once for the first Adam and teaches that the Cross was a one- time deal. Why would God allow another go around with FW? It didn't work the first time and would not the second. Keep in mind that Adam, before he fell, did not need Jesus. He was sinless. After the Fall, Genesis 3:22 tells us "Then the Lord God said, Behold, the man has become like one of Us, knowing good from evil; and now, lest he stretch out his hand, and take also from the tree of life, and eat, and live forever". This is unequivocal that after the Fall, God's restrictions on Adam and thus our FW was severe. Combine this with the other context in Genesis like expulsion from the Garden, toil, domestic stress, etc., to get a picture of bondage to sin. In its original form, FW belonged to a sinless Adam. It would be wrong to argue that this kind of FW could continue after the Fall because the above scripture tells us we are dead. Jesus did not make us possessors of a FW like Adam's, but on the contrary, he made us bond servants. We are forever bonded to Christ. Adam was not. There is no way to make Paul's description of a servant fit the description of Adam's FW. Just one of many rebuttals to this "fit", Paul describes his role tempered with his sin nature while Adam had no sin nature.

Luther and Calvin were about the same age and lived in adjoining countries but did not collaborate. Luther attempted to correspond with Calvin but he refused. Some narrators attribute this to a personality clash. Calvin was introverted and reserved and Luther was loud and uncouth. Luther's book was a masterpiece esoterically. At that time, his

> "We did not make this world and we don't have any control over its events."
> SPOKEN BY WOODROW WILSON, THE UNDISPUTED MOST DEVOUT U. S. PRESIDENT WHILE MAKING THE DECISION TO DECLARE ENTRY INTO WW1, SOUNDING LIKE HE THOUGHT FW WAS NOT A CHOICE.

treatment and teachings on bondage could not be equaled and many of today's theologians use his book as a template and his "Bondage of the Will" remains a classic example of a head on refutation of FW. Calvin's "*Institutes…*" has no equal in its depth and scope of systematic examination of the Bible. But Calvin did not address the bondage issue as detailed and forcibly as did Luther. Luther and Calvin deserve as much praise as the other church Martyrs, even those who died defending their faith. Although not burned at the stake, Calvin had to escape death by fleeing France. Luther escaped death while standing his ground and defying the church tribunal and not recanting his testimony. Luther is known as the Father of The Protestant Reformation who wrested the Protestant Church from the power of the great Roman Catholic Church that had ruled all of Europe for centuries since the time of the Apostles. After Calvin died, his followers wanted to simplify the complexity of "*The Institutes …*" and developed an acronym called TULIP. This was needed in order to refute the Arminian theology that taught, and is still being taught, FW. This marks the beginning of the modern-day chasm between FW believers and Calvinism. When I started this book, I did not realize this chasm can be represented by mostly one issue, FW.

Based on this assessment, I claim that FW is the cornerstone theology of the majority of the western denomination churches. A church's FW theology arguably is what holds that church together more than any other factor, yet is never spoken of or taught in the theological sense like saving grace, atonement, or the many other doctrines.

There are several benefits to knowing that FW is fake news. One is it would throw the brakes on the insistence to be one hundred percent self-reliant. I am referring to those Christians who believe that the blood of Christ must be joined with their works to attain salvation. And it will foster the realization that we need more prayer time because of the increase in the complexity of our life styles. It will enable us to realize that we are not in as much control as we thought we were by taking that control away from FW and placing it where it should be. The other benefit is we can become more in tune with God's sovereignty. A person can remain a FWer yet at the same time believe that his FW is not as potent as he thought it was. This at least is an improvement. The above is listed as a possibility of benefits, possibilities that I doubt will occur. A belief in FW has survived for centuries. I believe the majority of those who believe in Luther's bondage of the will, Calvinism, also will not experience some of the above benefits. There is a difference in believing something and practicing it and it is hard to increase one's faith sometimes, as evidenced by Paul's testimony that he does those things that he doesn't want to do. At times, I don't practice it and I am just being real. Most people on either side of the fence do not care about the science that tells us our subconscious minds mostly control our behavior or care about the difference between FW and Calvinistic bondage. I believe that most Christians will not increase their devotion to God by devoting more time to theological issues. A stronger fellowship with God is personal and there is nothing personal in theology. All Christians benefit from having a personal relationship with God, regardless of theology and denomination. We would do well to dwell on Solomon's wisdom, Ecclesiastes 1:18, "Because in much wisdom there is much grief, and increasing knowledge results in increasing pain." He gives us hope in 7:8: "The end of a thing is better than its beginning."

In addition to the benefits previously discussed, there may be another benefit to knowing FW is fake. There is a saying that if it is not broken, don't fix it. It must be considered that our American genius for adaptation, represented by Henry Ford and others, may be taking another "flight of the Phenix". Some people may have the same questions about FW as I do but instead of throwing the baby out with the wash and moving into the Calvinistic camp, they have attempted a fix by changing its definition. These people understand the principle of cause and effect as well as I do and may have modified FW by removing some of its free characteristics and mixing in some compromises. I claim this is not far-fetched by citing a recent medical advance in which some forms of cancer in a trial study are being successfully stopped by injecting a polio virus directed into the cancer cells. A redefined FW could encompass the belief that we're free to the extent that something in our brain not yet understood permits a compatible "handshake" for lack of a better word, between our conscious and unconscious minds. This is being discussed in some scientific circles.

There are two aspects of bondage of the will. One relates to salvation and is controlled by God's sovereignty. The other is how our will relates to our daily actions and behavior and is controlled by environmental and genetic factors but it must be remembered that both these factors are also influenced by God since He has caused everything, beginning with "Let there be light." When comparing salvation according to the FW belief and to Calvinism, the inequity should be apparent, but to the FWer, it is not. Jim supposedly has FW and <u>Jim's choice</u> of becoming saved depends first on FW and secondly on God's permission. But the problem here is that God must have the primary role. In this scenario, FW teaches that Jim's choice takes precedence over God's choice. To initiate FW salvation, his ability to choose must come from within himself, meaning his choice cannot be fettered by outside influences. This means that God is unable to save him until he gives God permission. There is nothing secure about gaining his salvation or maintaining it. It's unbelievable how

> *"Man can live by bread alone if its kneaded with five daily fruits of the Spirit."*
> SAM SHIPLEY

FWers describe FW as a two-way street, going into eternal life or going out. Becoming saved would be risky in the FW world as it attempts to trample and soil the many scriptures that explain that salvation must be sealed with security. Christ said that no one can take from Him what God has given. In comparison, John is saved by <u>God's choice.</u> Of the above two choices, which do you think is biblical, is the easiest, and provides eternal security? Let's examine another scenario. Joe and Jack were twin brothers. Both were exposed to the same childhood and adulthood environments. Assuming that FW exists, Joe died saved and Jack died lost. Why did God permit Jack to get the short end of the stick? Hint. It could not be because Joe's FW made him wiser or more spiritually discerning because FW is claimed to be an innate trait present at birth and if so, this would make it a genetic inheritance which in turn would make FW a fettered force which Jack did not have. If Joe's "edge" was not genetic, this would mean that his advantage was gained from his environment. If this was the case, it would cancel out FW. Part of the answer lies in Matthew 7:23. "And I will declare to them, I never knew you; depart from Me, you who practice lawlessness." And in Romans 8:27. "...because He intercedes for the saints according to the will of God." And Romans 9:16. "So then it does not depend on the man who wills or the man who runs, but on God who has mercy." Our choices, actions, and behavior are not a product of our own making but are the product of someone or something outside the sphere of our control, whether that be God, spouse or friend, or a stoplight that did not stay green long enough. If I run a red light, it would elicit a specific set of behaviors, none of which should be attributed to FW, but they are. We don't become angry because we freely choose to. Anger is caused by something outside ourselves.

There are too many factors that interfere with and override what we think is our conscious unfettered decision making. There is no such thing as an unfettered decision. You can't sweep aside the way you were raised and say your decisions are not caused by family ties. You can't control your family's ties to the Catholic Church. If you become a Catholic, your ties to your family are probably one of the causes, although there can be others. If you don't become a Catholic, there was a cause that caused this. And this cause also was not orchestrated by you. The easy way to understand causes is to use the domino effect. It takes one domino acting as the primary causer and the other dominos acting like effects. Maybe a friend got you interested in another church. You can't control the influence your friend has on you whether it be good or bad. Your standards for how you perceive your friends or world is a learned process as you were growing up. It's attributed to your upbringing and your environment. You can't control who your friends are. If you and your friend have a fight and you decide to end the relationship, this will not be an example of a decision caused by FW. It will be a decision caused by the fight. You could argue that you freely had a fight but this would not be honest or logical. Something caused you to have a fight. You didn't cause yourself. You met Jim in the third grade and he is your lifelong friend but your parents caused you to be in the third grade and they are who caused you to meet him. You can't control the reason you like Jim. You liked Jim not because you initially said "I am going to like Jim"

> *"Democracy is the worst form of government. Except for all others."*
> WINSTON CHURCHILL

but because something prompted you to like him and you were not the cause of that prompt.

Things in your past guide your future. I can claim this because of the principle of cause and effect. Cause and effect is diametrically opposed to FW. The FW argument teaches that a person can originate a cause from within himself and make a decision that is irrelevant to the causes coming from outside himself. We can't cause ourselves to do anything without the help of outside stimuli any more than we can cause our autonomic nervous system to cause us to breathe. If I decide to open the door, I have to have a reason and this reason does not originate solely from my FW, which allegedly resides in my brain. I don't just say "I will open the door". Anything we do is caused by stimuli from outside the realm of FW. The cause that makes me go to work did not come from FW. The reason I go to work every day is caused by my mortgage and my family. If I could freely choose to not go, I wouldn't go. It's impossible for me to do any thing freely because of the many extenuating circumstances, because of my fettered life. We have all heard about people who love their jobs so much and never retire and base this longevity on their ability to freely choose what they want to do. I believe they do love their jobs but let's examine this to see if FW is the driving force, to see if they can freely choose to work or not work or if there is an underlying cause that control's their love for their job. God's agape love is the mother of all love. Scripture tells us "because he first loved us." Were it not for his love, this world would have never survived. The love of each of us for others comes from Him. The hate that caused Cain to kill his brother came from Satan. Let's see if what they love is only their jobs. I claim that these people were born with a strong urge, penchant, to always stay busy and loved busyness before they ever started work at their jobs. We all have this urge but some have it more so. However, it is possible they began work to pay the mortgage and found a job they really loved. No matter which category they are in, FW has no part to play. If they love their job, something caused them to love it and it did not come from within themselves. We don't love without a reason or cause and it is impossible for a person to have an innate love that came from within himself. However, since Christ is in us, it is His love the world sees. A person won't be able to freely quit the job he loves unless something overrides this love, unless something stronger than love causes this love to be cancelled out. If their compulsion to stay busy continues, they can't freely choose to quit until a stronger compulsion to quit overrides the compulsion to stay.

Cause and effect is the principle set in motion when God created the universe and subsequently us. Our human design is built on this principle, much like the cohesion of the universe is built on and caused by gravity. The smallest particle to the largest mass obediently follows God's design. The clay we were created from to the living tissue of our bodies follows the dictates of His grand design. Cause and effect is a stand-alone principle that governs

> "It is impossible to rightly govern the world without God and the Bible."
> GEORGE WASHINGTON

everything. A decision or action made today can be caused, not by a conscious and stand-alone act of FW, but by a cause that originated in the past that resides in our subconscious mind and is just now bearing fruit. This is proven by research addressed in this book that shows that ninety-five percent of our behavior is caused by our subconscious minds. Our subconscious mind is the driving force behind our behavior. It's overwhelming and praiseworthy of God that He designed such a magnificent creature as Man. Our subconscious mind is indelible. It is said an elephant doesn't forget anything. Its brain is four time the size of ours but we have something better than size. Even with fewer neurons, our brain has the ability to know and worship God and it's this transcendency that makes us His divine kinship. The most thrilling discovery I made since becoming a Christian was it does not matter whether you are in the scientific world of Einstein's or Freud's or the spiritual world of Luther's, Calvin's, or Augustine's, God's world demands that cause and effect is what governs the behavior of Man and the universe. I claim that cause and effect is the mother of our behavior and God is the Father. The Bible has proof of cause and effect on every page and it proves the psychological axiom of "Give me your child until the age of five and I will give you back the adult he will become." The Bible tells us that when we impart Bible teachings when a child is young, he will not depart from it and this is true concerning all teachings.

Nothing happens by chance and everything has a purpose. On the other hand, FW is touted as something that originates by chance, depending on what a free will choice is that is on the table. It teaches that I can choose God depending on what I think about God today or not choose Him tomorrow, depending on what I am thinking then. This is a direct and flagrant affront to the scripture that states "just as He chose us in Him before the foundation of the world…." in Ephesians 1:4. Did God chose me before the foundation and then forget me when I rejected Him? Romans 8:29 states "For those whom He foreknew…." This is interpreted by FW theology to mean that God looked ahead, saw the direction I was going to take, and yielded to my direction, or FW choice. Calvinism teaches that He determined the direction I was going to take and this was the reason He foreknew my direction. God does not use His foreknowledge to determine what will happen. What will happen is determined beforehand. In coming to grips with why God determines, foreknows, and allows anything is a project that everyone should pursue all the way to its end in order to have a peace of mind that surpasses all understanding. What caused WWII where fifty million people died, and why, or what caused a mere little sparrow to fall are questions that will go unanswered without knowledge of divine sovereignty and human bondage, and of all the dominations and theologies in the world, Calvinism is the only one that offers biblical proof of the answers while at the same time, confessing and acknowledging ignorance of why God chooses some for election but not others, except to explain it is because of His mercy and grace. Calvin's answer is the biblical answer. Paul tells us it is a mystery except to say that it is the will of God through His mercy. What enhances my assurance regarding the mysteries of God is the lockstep between Calvinism and science. Calvinism and reformed theology are the only churches that agree with both science and the Bible. Science is the expression of God as reflected in the majesty of the universe.

This book is not a fatalistic discussion on how we are not responsible for our actions or how we are not morally accountable. Responsibility and accountability cannot be ignored or denied just because I had no *conscious* control over something I did not *remember causing*. It's been proven that our conscious ability to guide our thoughts and behavior is sorely lacking but this does not obviate our accountability. A study conducted by Masao Matsuhashi and Mark Hallett in 2008, entitled *The timing of the conscious intention to move,* and reported in *The European Journal of Neuroscience,* found that individual neurons fired two seconds before the subject reported his intention to act. Some scientists questioned the accuracy of the timing in other similar studies but this is how the scientific method works, to conduct endless follow up research and question every aspect. Hundreds of other studies have confirmed that the event occurred before conscious awareness. Matsuhashi and Hallett summarize their study thusly: "If our conscious intentions are what causes movement genesis, then naturally our conscious intentions should always occur before any movement has begun. Otherwise, if we become aware of a movement only after it has already been started, our awareness could not have been the cause of that particular movement. Simply put, conscious intention must precede action if it is its cause." One researcher, John Dylan Hayes, states: "How can I call a will mine if I don't even know when it occurred and what it has decided to do?" In regards to responsibility and accountability, this is what the Holy Spirit is for, bringing to our conscious mind those things that will teach us God's will and the difference between right and wrong and give us the ability to discern the difference. This is what I pray, "that His will be done," not my FW. This Book contains proof that we are not aware of the majority of causes in our life. When God brings these unconscious causes to our attention, we are responsible to be cooperative. God caused me to be saved but I have the responsibility to cooperate with His cause. If my upbringing caused me to live a life of crime, I am responsible to God to

> "For whom He foreknew He also foreordained to be conformed to the image of His Son, that He might be the first born among many brothern, and whom He foreknew, them He also called; and whom He called, them He also justified; and who He justified, them He also glorified."
>
> ROMANS 8:29-30

cooperate and reject my environment but I must give God credit for my ability to corporate. Love is what caused me to marry but since I am incapable of agape love by way of FW, the cause belongs to God. All good things come from God and even my ability to corporate comes from Him. We must be quick to thank God for two reasons; one is thanking Him for a good thing, and the other is thanking Him for the ability to recognize what a good thing is. This Book is an attempt to explain the difference between causation and cooperation. If this Book succeeds in showing you what real freedom is, you will be able to depend more on God and less on FW. This is not easy to do because it requires giving up a freedom we really don't have and replacing it with Christ's. Do not let this dishearten you. The road to final redemption (not salvation) is traveled in inches, not leaps and bounds. I am still moving along, slowly but surely. Instead of claiming credit for my FW ability to choose a friend, I must cooperate with God to see Who is the real Chooser. If my friend was God's choice, our relationship will prosper. If my choice was not God's choice, the relationship will suffer. I have the ability to make a bad choice, but bad choices in our lives are caused by Satan who uses FW to his advantage.

In this book, you will read about one project that proves that 95 percent of everything we do is caused by our subconscious mind. The conscious/subconscious research projects addressed in this book were published for the public and do not include details and their brevity prompts questions. Much of the details are mine and some of them may not be specifically proven by research

> "*Keep your eyes wide open before marriage, half shut after.*"
> BEN FRANKLIN

but nevertheless are sound logical inferences. The core conclusions of these research projects are scientifically sound and my extraneous details are a reasonable extension. A fettered decision can be caused by watching a current TV ad that is sending a subliminal prompt acting directly on our conscious mind. An example is I buy a tube of Crest toothpaste. One reason I think I bought it is because I like the taste, which is true. But taste is the secondary cause. The primary cause is the unseen prompts. This can be proven by the efficacy of subliminal advertising, which spends millions daily. Another proof is people will buy something that has a neutral taste because of a sneaky prompt and is bought entirely because of the prompt. Another example nullifying FW is I buy Crest toothpaste without being exposed to sublimation merely because I like the taste. This purchase would not be an exercise in FW and is scientifically ruled out because I don't have FW control over my taste buds. I can't control what I like or don't like unless I employ mind changing therapy and this would obviate FW as a primary cause. It's true I can override my taste buds but this would require a cause that is not associated with FW. I don't override my taste buds without a reason, and science is proving that reasons for choices do not come from FW. My taste buds are a genetic cause for something I like and as you will see in this book, cause is the motivator and force that determines what my taste preferences are. I can't freely decide to like mint, choose a church, the kind of car I like, etc. I am not saying I can't control my behavior when I don't like something. I am saying I can't stop disliking something without being influenced by something outside myself, outside my FW. If I am influenced to change my behavior by therapy, FW cannot be a factor. Dislike would be what causes me to change my behavior. I can't freely choose to dislike something without a reason (cause) or do something unless I am mind control programmed by an outside agent. It's true I can overcome my taste and buy something else, maybe because it's cheaper. But this would be a different scenario and the same rules apply. It cheapness was the cause and I don't have control over its cheapness or control over wanting to save money. In determining the validity of FW, what I did, not what I could have done, determines the actual cause of my action. Hypothetical choices are irrelevant and don't become a choice until the decision is made. Things I hypothetically could have done must be considered when I do them and considered on their own merits and they too

> *"J have the body of a god.....*
> *Buddha" Bumper sticker*
> SEEN ON A BUMPER STICKER

would have causes. The definition of FW (defined by both the FW believers and the dictionary) demands that the freedom to choose must be characterized by conscious *and unencumbered choice.* If its encumbered and influenced strongly enough by someone or something that causes a decision to be made, the choice was made by someone or something other than themselves and was made through them acting as an inter-mediator. FWers frequently use the argument that when I am subliminally exposed to an advertisement and I don't buy anything, this proves the validity of FW. I don't have to buy anything to prove that sublimity works. Sublimity, like anything else in life, is based on and works because of cause and effect. It's not a gun to my head. Sublimity is proven when I buy something because I am not aware of what caused me to buy it, and conversely, when I don't buy something, it was because of something in the past which caused my dislike and which was caused by something outside my realm of control. I and my FW, of ourselves, did not cause anything. FW requires that I can buy it or not and the choice is made regardless of outside influences but nothing happens in the absence of outside influences. We are not in a vacuum that is obvious to external influences. It's true that I can ignore an advertisement but that only means there was a cause for why I ignored it. I didn't need toothpaste, something distracted me, or my wife had already bought some. Another proof is people will buy something that has a neutral taste and logic dictates that the purchase must have a cause. You will never see a person standing in front of a Crest display and flipping a coin but if you did, that means the person has a penchant for gambling, in which case the penchant would be the cause.

FW believers give genes their due credit when it comes to physical attributes. I know I have blue eyes because both my Father and his Father had them. But other attributes such as IQ that have an effect on our behavior, and thus our will, are not given due credit by FWers. The genetic aspects of taste buds are also not considered by a FW believer as justified grounds for trashing FW. But it should be because taste buds are not controlled by FW. (It's an autonomic process) Changes in taste cannot be accomplished by FW. A person cannot freely choose to like strawberry better than chocolate. Some tastes are inherited and some tastes are manipulated by clever advertisements that make us think we like or dislike something. In manipulation, change is made in the brain and not in the tongue, which is to say the taste bud does not change. It must be noted that both FW believers and the dictionary define FW as an act that was made *without* unfettered influence and *with* full control and manipulation by the actor. Yet FWers ignore this definition because it encroaches on their personal freedom. It's as if FWers accept this definition but don't either understand its meaning or don't accept its ramifications but I think the most likely reason is a refusal to apply the scientific principle of cause and effect to theology and things of the Church. The average person is prone to believe that everyday mundane things should not be explained with the complexity of science. Life is too complicated so keep it simple. This is much like the Newtonian era when people refused to give up the simple flat earth belief and replace it with the complex idea that global dimensions cannot be measured in straight linear fashion. FW today is fake news that people refuse to give up. The reason it's in the dictionary is because of its common use, not because of its scientific viability or its correct usage.

When I answer the phone or do any of thousands of acts, FW Christians say that it was my free will, unaided by any influences outside myself that caused me to answer. They will say that since I could answer or not answer, that proves I have FW. Not so. It's true that I chose to answer, but I did not freely choose. Someone or something else compelled me to answer. I was taught and caused to answer the phone and this teaching did not originate in me or my will. If you put a child, or adult for that matter, who has not been taught that a ringing phone needs to be answered, they will not answer in order to talk to someone. They won't know there is someone there to talk to. They may pick the phone up out of curiosity but this is not a free action but an action caused by an innate and genetic trigger, a trigger that cannot be consciously and self- initiated (but it can be overridden, to be discussed later). Curiosity is one of the causes that brought us out of the cave. We were designed and caused to have curiosity. We did not cause ourselves to be curious. If you want to say I was not compelled but merely influenced, it is still not FW. You can say I could have freely chose to not answer the phone. No. If I had not answered, something would have caused me to not answer. I would have been compelled to not answer in the same way that I was compelled to answer. Both to answer or not answer was dictated by a force(s) that was not my FW. Maybe I had something on the stove that caused me to not answer. I am not going to answer or not answer without a reason, a cause.

Keep in mind that this petty give and take argument regarding freedom and choices is necessary because FW believers claim that a choice can be made via FW solely on their FW power without being influenced to a degree that would require their choice to be different. FWers refuse to accept any outside extenuating circumstances that play a major role in decision making. This is important because a FW believer

> "*All men are animals, some just make better pets.*"
> BUMPER STICKER

claims he can choose God without any help from God or anyone else. Even if God told them they were going to lose their soul if they did not accept Him, they can freely reject Him. There is nothing free about this. It requires a cause to both accept or reject God. The FW believer acknowledges that God is available if he needs any help and he has heard the Word preached many times but he believes his decision is immune to any fettered influences. But science has proven that everything has a cause or compulsion or force and every cause or compulsion or force has an effect. It's becoming more and more difficult to find an event or action that originates within "self", according to science. And not only is 95 percent of our actions caused by something outside our conscious self, the effect of 5 percent of our actions that are visible or conscious are seen poorly. "For now we see in a mirror dimly…" (1 Corinthians 13:12). Paul has to be referring to our consciousness because we sometimes can't even remember to bring home milk after work. It's a double whammy when a blind and deaf man is attempting to understand what caused a noise and is unable to see or hear its effect. But a FW believer thinks an unsaved person's spiritual discernment is the same as post-fall Adam's. The Bible teaches that a lost man is blind and deaf to the gospel the same as a physically blind and deaf man's loss of sight and sound. The FW belief tries to

> "*Earth is the insane asylum for the universe.*"
> BUMPER STICKER

teach that a lost man can come to God without God's help. The term bondage of the will was used by Martin Luther and reserved primarily for usage in a religious context to prove that we are either enslaved to sin and Satan is our master or in bondage to Christ as Paul was but he also used it in conjunction with secular behavior and did so without the benefit of science, cause and effect, or knowledge of the unconscious mind. Luther was ahead of his time and unintentionally used the Bible to prove what we now see science proving. When speaking of bondage, Luther unintentionally indicted modern civilization's addiction to cars, golf, or fishing. Paul said he did what he did not want to do. This enslavement or bondage relates to both spiritual and secular issues and to both bondage to Satan and bondage to Christ. Material and spiritual bondage is in force all the time and this time frame is constant but the objects and causes of this bondage change according to the culture and dynamics of the time. We can't be in bondage sometimes and not in other times. If I give up my addiction to golf, something else will take its place. God designed us to be active and not in a vacuum of nothingness. Going back to the pre-fall Garden, Adam had his pastimes by playing with his animals and exploring his Garden but his addictions didn't come until after the Fall. This is proven by God telling him that he could do anything except eat from the tree. It can't get any more free than that. All the above factors have a corresponding effect that relegate our behavior. Luther's treatment of a spiritually bound "will" relates to the chains of Satan in regards to a lost person or the irresistible and binding arms of Christ in regards to a Christian. A FW Christian just believes he can do things freely that he actually can't do. Luther's Bible teachings explains why I chose Christ. In effect, God chose me and only then could I choose Him, exemplifying cause and effect. Paul said he was a bond servant of Christ. From this, Luther paraphrased the term bondage. The correct interpretation of Paul's "bond servant" was that he was willfully bound to Christ.

Thirty vets commit suicide daily. Thirty thousand people commit suicide annually. Up to the age of twenty-four, four to five thousand deaths are from suicide annually. Of these, only six hundred and thirty-two were girls in 2003 as reported by U.S News and World Report. For teens, the lower brain, the amygdala, is where fear, anger, and depression are processed. Brain imaging studies show us that in suicidal people, levels of serotonin are too low. It is still being investigated if low levels of serotonin cause depression or depression cause low levels of serotonin. Regardless of how this turns out, this suggests that if a teenager loses his girlfriend and commits suicide, it was not primarily caused by depression but caused by something that caused depression, which is a domino effect chain of events. This shows that FW is not the causal agent. This alone, without regard to the hundreds of similar studies, shows that we have many mitigating unseen, unknown, and influential forces that shape and carve our behavior. In addition to these genetic causes, the environmental effects of the first five formative years must be considered and throughout life, neither our genetic code or our brain structure is static. Age and environmental factors cause our brain to shrink. Imaging of a teenage brain show that his brain structure has not fully developed. Text books of human physiology tell us that during the teenage years and through the twenties, the brains of this group are still developing and enlarging. Although not stated specifically, this informs that as additional neurons and pathways are added, a teenager's behavior is coached or influenced by new brain growth exactly like the behavior of a two-year-old will change at three years of age. Unconscious behavior is at work. These are the danger years when a teen's unconscious mind is adjusting to his conscious mind and acclimating itself to the strenuous chore of adjustment. This speaks to the same thing happening in a baby's brain in which his behavior can in no way be attributed to FW. It's bothersome that a FWer will acknowledge a baby's lack of conscious control yet claim that at age thirteen, children miraculously can begin to exercise their FW. They are saying that a thirteen-year old's age gave him time to grow his FW, even though at age four, he didn't have any. FW can't be exercised at any age. What people should be saying is that at age thirteen, teenagers' understanding of their awareness has increased, not their FW. An adult (teenagers were not used in the study) operates ninety-five percent of the time based on subconscious stimuli. In regards to abnormal behavior caused by

> *"Grow your own dope.*
> *Plant a man."*
> BUMPER STICKER

the environment, testimony before Congress has shown that the nerve gas saran has caused irreversible brain damage that will affect our vet's behavior for a lifetime and Post Traumatic Stress Disorder (PTSD) is also a lifelong disease. Suicide, depression, and the effects of trauma all stand as witness against FW. FWers give credence to the fact that FW may not play a part in suicidal situations but what is inexplicable is their belief that it plays a huge role in nonclinical aspects of everyday behavior and decision making. A suicidal person and a non-suicidal person share the same exact parameters of mind and brain activities. Just because someone is depressed or suicidal does not mean the conscious or unconscious functions of his mind/brain operate differently than that of someone who is not suicidal. Stated another way, a suicidal person's will was not made suicidal because of FW. Depression and other diseases are controlled or influenced by non-FW factors. Mental health experts confirm that suicide is a disease and can't be treated as if FW was the originating and primary cause. New research in neurology is showing that everyone should be assessed based on the relationship between conscious and unconscious behavior. I have little information as to when or if this research is being used in the mental health community.

An article in the U.S. News and World Report, September 2003 issue, written by David G. Grimm, reports that many of our adult diseases such as high blood pressure, diabetes, obesity, heart disease, and osteoporosis have their origin in the womb. When combining this with what we know about genetic inheritance, it doesn't leave much room for freedom within the FWers choice ranges. A person born with an IQ of one hundred and a genetic predisposition of high blood pressure is not on the same level playing field as someone born with a silver spoon in his mouth and has a higher IQ and no disabilities but God's plan of salvation (as taught by Calvinism) offsets this uneven playing field. God's choices for salvation are based on His mysterious criteria which does not consider our choices or works. Calvinism does not claim to know why God exercises His mercy and grace on some but not others. Calvinism is criticized for teaching that God saves us even though we don't want to be saved at first. Genesis 3:3 tells us that Adam would die if he ate the forbidden fruit. This tells us plainly that a spiritually dead person is incapable of wanting God until God intervenes because as soon as he ate the fruit, he hid from God. God intervenes with some at an early age. FW teaches that salvation is based on a person's FW, which is capricious and changes from hour to hour and remains unstable his entire life. This is the FWer's characterization, not mine, although they do not use the negative term "capricious". I am not exaggerating when I say that FW theology boasts of the flexibility of FW. The ability to choose is its hallmark and flagship. It would be unfair of God if He did the choosing and disallowed free choice in the matter, they say. FW teaches that when we are born, our fate is in our hands. I am not overstating when I say that having FW is like throwing dice. You never know what's coming up. You can become secure in God for the moment but like Job, we can lose all our possessions, see our family die, be criticized by the community, and have boils and sores over our bodies. This could be enough for some people to reject God's salvation as taught by FW. But it's impossible for the elect and chosen to reject Him and Job proves this. If anyone in the history of the Bible had a FW reason to reject God, it would have been Job. Based on many documentaries, people claim to give God up because of their bitterness when a spouse dies or they lose their job and cancer strikes but I claim that the primary reason in rejecting God is God's rejection. FW teaches that God does not interfere with the human playing field, meaning that God gave us FW so that we could be the interveners and like Darwinism, leaves salvation up to the survival of the fittest. This is because, they say, God gave us FW so that we could come freely to Him and not be drawn to Him in a manner we could not refuse. They interpret God's

> "Stupidity often saves a man from going mad."
> OLIVER WENDELL HOLMES JR.

irresistible grace to be a claim that it would make God a trespasser. If your FW is strong, you will survive. If it's weak, you will vacillate between Heaven and Hell. This is an unbelievable FW position. When God chooses a person with an IQ of eighty, He does not depend on that person's ability to make a salvation decision (without His help) and does not relegate FW as that person's pathway to salvation. God's plan of salvation has nothing to do with FW and everything to do with His irresistible grace. Paul nicknamed this grace bondage when he said he was a bond servant. Calvinism teaches that irresistible grace is what makes God's playing field level. FW, if it existed, makes the playing field skewed in favor of those who have a stronger FW. The foundation of FW is built on humanistic control and everyone could be saved if he was willing. FW teaches that a Muslim can become a Christian solely through the auspices of FW and without any earthly or divine influence. FW has been inserted into our democratic form of government but as research has shown, it is not scientifically accepted there.

I am going to show how the Bible's principle of bondage of the will and science's principle of cause and effect share the same characteristics. Paul describes himself as a bond servant and describes other Christians in the same light. The blood of Christ was the cause and bondage its effect. Science's entire premise is based on cause and effect. Take John Calvin's advice and don't jump ship until you read what science is saying about our will. It is interesting to me to know the real reason I was saved, got promoted, or why I married who I did. The majority of people believe in FW as a church doctrine and how it serves as a guide that explains both our secular and spiritual behavior. But this majority has been taught grievously wrong. However, knowing the truth about what causes us to behave the way we do will not change the way we behave. If everyone believed that the subconscious mind tells the conscious mind what to do, as proven in research, it would not affect our behavior. But what should change is our knowledge of God's sovereignty. FW is taught as the freedom to choose God before God chooses you. He waits for you to choose Him and He seconds the motion and then chooses you, they say. FW allegedly gives you the power to reject God but a FWer can think this even though God first chose him. This teaching denigrates God and makes His Sovereignty subject to our sovereignty. But if you will think about it, we Christians do a dozen things daily that denigrates Him. A wonderful example is Peter's denial of Christ three times and not once during that terrible night did he regain his faith. FW is a security blanket that some Christians need that gives the security needed to get through life because of the feeling of control that it gives and the power to control one's destiny. I acknowledge this one benefit of FW but claim there is a better way. It seems contradictory to say that the FW myth has a benefit. Proverbs 3:5-6 is the better way. "Trust in the Lord with all your heart and do not lean on your own understanding. In all your ways acknowledge Him and He will make your paths straight." He wants us to feel secure but He wants us to realize that He is our blanket. He does not want us to feel fearful and uncertain. He wants Christians to feel free but not through the power of their FW. He wants us to make Him the source of our freedom, **the source of** our **control.** But God tolerates FW. When God chooses a person, His mind is made up. We can know for a fact that God is a pursuer by reading the many testimonies that tell us that they were saved late in life. The Bible calls those who are chosen the elect, meaning they did not elect themselves and teaches that the elect can confirm his/her Christian status. Bondage of the will, for a Christian, is not a prison but rather an escape from Satan's prison, an escape from the penalty of sin. Calvinists believe in the principle of bondage as a Church doctrine but don't give it much thought and Calvinist pastors very seldom teach it. But it needs to be pointed out how the idea of FW came to hold such a prominent and popular position in our American culture and government and then how it transposed and inserted itself into church doctrine in both Calvinist and FW churches in an attempt to invalidate the biblical doctrine of bondage of the will.

Students of the evolution of Calvinism in America and American history will find that the Calvinistic Puritans came from England to escape the religious persecution of the Church of England. In 1534, King Henry separated the Church of England from the Roman Catholic Church in Rome, resulting in a Church-State entity with the State (England) riding herd over the affairs of the Church. The Church therefore existed in a culture of bondage to the State. The Founding Fathers made sure this would not happen in their new America, thus creating the separation of Church and State and ensuring freedom from civil bondage. Patrick Henry said "Give me liberty or give me death." In my opinion, the hue and cry of civil freedom began to mix with and affect the beliefs regarding spiritual bondage

> *"Dopamine neurons are responsible for telling the rest of the brain what stimulus to pay attention to."*
> TERRY SEJNOWSKI IN HIS RESEARCH PROVING THAT THE UNCONSCIOUS MIND RULES

taught by the Calvinists and in this mix, the FW stepchild was born in America. In addition, the colonial population grew as did the churches that did not teach bondage (FW teachers), causing an oxymoron, in effect, Church bondage attempting to live in harmony with civil freedom. The two do not mix well. This dis-harmony or disconnect took time to develop but as proof, even modern-day Calvinistic churches barely give lip service to any kind of bondage theology even though this represents the founding principle of Calvinism in Europe which was brought to our early colonies. Calvinism has now become the stepchild put in the closet and kept out of sight. And the non-bondage denominations grew in size and popularity and taught FW. America cherishes freedom of all kinds more than any other country, freedom to choose God, civil freedom, and this is why a belief in FW prospered during the later colonial period. But the Puritans (non-FW) were devout Calvinists and church historians place them as being more instrumental in establishing moral principles in the Colonies than any other group. The Calvinistic footprint is unmistakable in the Founding Fathers blueprint that established our Constitution. I am amazed at how little even well -read people know about the lasting benefits that were created by the Calvinistic Puritans. Calvinists founded two or three colleges. Bondage of the will theology, in its early formation and especially later, did not receive as warm a welcome in the Colonies as it did in Europe, except for its ardent followers. Bondage of the will is biblically valid and the interpretative exegesis of Scripture supporting or denying its validity has changed little except for a few curves in the road (but with no major changes in direction) and with little change in theological and denominational acceptance. But our culture has changed dramatically. A side note is there are about twenty-seven or eight scriptures that defend Calvinism and about the same number that defend non-Calvinist (FW) theology. Calvinistic theology uses a wide range of methods to invalidate the FW argument. One example is John 3:16, the flagship of the FW "fleet." "For God so loved the world that He gave His only …" The word "world" used in this context, say the Calvinists, cannot mean every individual person in the world, thus invalidating the belief, at least in this one scripture, that Christ died for every person. But even if He did die for everyone, many FW Christians along with Calvinists, believe that His death was atonement for only some people. Welcome to the beginning of the argument that has gone on for centuries with no end in sight. I say "beginning" because there are many issues in this age-old argument. As our culture has changed, so has our religious beliefs and this cultural change has been toxic to our biblical doctrine. One example of how culture trumps religion can be seen vividly in Calvin's day. At that time, any man or woman who challenged the authority of the Church must be put to death. Calvin was on a committee in charge of safeguarding the Church's authority. Calvin was careful in keeping doctrine separate from culture because everything in his "Institutes …" is based on sound biblical exegesis. He voted to behead the accused. But he thought of this as housekeeping and not doctrine; today we would call it doctrine. This was traditional Church practice and he treated keeping order in the Church much like sweeping the floor. Luther was exposed to the same necessity of keeping house. In Calvin's France (he moved to Sweden) it was the guillotine. In Luther's Germany, it was burning at the stake. One example of over jealous tradition that had a negative impact on biblical truth was the Salem Witch-Hunts. Another example of a widely distributed geographical cultural change occurring in the U.S. in modern times is known as Humanism. Carl Sagan, among others, defined this movement as, using my words for simplicity, an identity crisis. The personal pronoun "I" was defined as the most important word in the dictionary, so to speak. How a person felt or thought took precedence over what God thought. People who bought into this believed that God was here to serve us. I acknowledge that a person who believes in FW could be a Christian but Humanism is a tool used by many to prove that "I" can choose God before He chooses me and

> *"I took an IQ test and the results were negative."*
> BUMPER STICKER

"I" can reject God. Humanism is founded on the principle that people are the center of the universe. I am simply writing what the FW believers are themselves saying and writing, even though they may not think of FW as being Humanistic, it sounds like it. Another reason that Calvinism decreased and a belief in FW increased is Calvinism is not user friendly because of its intricacies and details contained in *The Institutes of the Christian Religion*. Bondage of the Will is the sister of predestination and is hard to accept and teaches that God chooses some and rejects others. My standard reply defending God as the chooser rather than FW as the chooser is, if you had a choice, wouldn't you rather have God doing the choosing? Romans 8:28 tells us "He called according to His purpose," which is only one scripture among many that support predestination but to be balanced, there are just as many that FWers use to disprove it. Sometimes we critique God by complaining that he does not give enough details and reasons for some of the things he does. This supposedly lack of reasons is a stumbling block that can be resolved by reading other mysteries of the Bible. But we must accept what is given. We cannot understand many mysteries even if He explained them. We would still be asking why. He told us plainly why he killed all the people in the world (or at least in the Middle East) except for Noah's family, yet we still ask Him why He didn't spare the infants and children. Some commentators use the "inherent sin" principle for the total destruction. Like many people, I was hoping to find something in the Book of Romans other than His mercy as a reason for His choosing. Why did He have mercy on me but not others? I ask this because of my firm belief that salvation is unconditional, i.e., neither I or anyone else can contribute to salvation. Why did He predestine some but not others? Why did He foreknow some but not others? I believe one of the reasons He took our FW away after the Fall was it would have enabled us to live forever without the power of the Cross, without the Blood of Christ. "Then the Lord God said, 'Behold the man has become like one of us, knowing good and evil: and now, lest he stretch out his hand, and take also from the tree of life, and eat, and live forever." (Gen. 3:22) And once I study through this mystery, as Paul calls it, I have to come to grips with understanding predestination. Calvinism is the most complex Christian theology in the western world. The majority of Protestant denominations, excluding the Reformed Churches, have doctrines less complicated than the Calvinist and Reformed Churches. These Protestant denominations claim they can explain why God chooses in two words, FW, and without acknowledging it, throw in mercy as an afterthought, depending on if FW wants to accept God's mercy. This relates to our modern-day mentality of the need to keep it short and sweet and our absolute demand to find an answer to all our problems and questions, even if we have to settle for unproven conjecture. If it's comfortable, wear it. If it's reasonable, use it. I acknowledge that FW is reasonable until its cover is removed. This is why FW is so attractive to the FW believer. They explain in two words what takes a Calvinist a book to explain. Calvin taught the simplicity of salvation but the complexity of God. Calvin taught that our mind, brain, body, soul, spirit, and God are too complex for us to know and understand some of the answers we demand. Paul says we are not fully redeemed and we see through a dark glass. (1 Corinthians 13:12) "For now I see in a mirror dimly, but then face to face; now I know in part but then I will know fully just as I also have been fully known." Calvin's, Paul's, and Luther's profound grasp of the Bible is amazing. When I was younger, I thought that men who studied and wrote books and commentary centuries ago were inspired but were old fogies. I thought that modern theologians had a big advantage in their research and writings because our computers, phones, Internet, social media, etc. gave us the ability to have a keener insight. But age and my own fogginess changed my mind on that. It took Calvin four years to write his book. And if he had had our technology, he could have completed it sooner. But the acumen and insight he brought to bear cannot be equaled today even with our technology.

In discussing behavior caused by genes, environment, or a mixture of both, let's look at each one individually. An example of genetic behavior in regards to a healthy person whose brain is physically intact is when a person is crying or depressed, the gene that triggered that behavior was stimulated by someone or something outside that person's zone of control. If it was triggered or controlled internally by FW, that would disqualify the gene or the

> *"Taxation with representation is not so hot either."*
> BUMPER STICKER

source of the external stimulus as being the cause of the depression. Obviously, this would destroy the science of inherited traits as established by Mendel's Law. It needs to be noted that depression and other emotional types of behavior are examples of dual causes. If someone yells at me, my genetic disposition or the way I was raised (environment) entices me to yell back. An example of environmentally caused behavior is when a person is walking on a sidewalk and for some reason he avoids stepping on the partition that separates each square. I used to do this and don't know why. My favorite personal environmentally caused behavior is I avoid running over even a small pebble. When I learned to drive, I hit a large rock and my Dad yelled at me and gave me a light slap on the back of the head. In discussing FW as it pertains to our secular behavior, its illogical construction is barely tolerable but when considering its spiritual ramifications, I have no tolerance for it. FWers define God as One who will not force Himself on anyone and that is true, He don't. God is like a black hole developing in space. He pulls you in and you want to be pulled in. FWers claim that we represent God as a trespasser who comes in without permission. In one sense of the word, this is true. All lost people at first resist, in varying degrees, God's offer. But if God wants you, He is capable of being irresistible. God is the Godfather who makes an offer that can't be refused, but the recipient does not want to refuse it. Calvinism calls it irresistible grace. God is the greatest Dealmaker and Artist of the deal, Trump notwithstanding. He can sell you real estate in Heaven and you won't know you bought anything, although you have an infinite title to the property. Rene Descartes, a French philosopher, said "I think. Therefore I am." This can be interpreted more than one way. He could have inadvertently meant that if a person thinks he has FW, he has it, regardless of factual evidence. I choose this meaning even though he did not specifically use the word "FW". His writings place him in the ranks of a FW believer, but one of his statements belies this, i.e., "Except our own thoughts, there is nothing absolutely in our power." This does not sound like someone who thinks FW is a fact. Or he could have been referring to a person who thinks he is rich, or will be rich, through the power of self-suggestion by invoking mind over matter. Cognition is the ability to think and reason and FW believers, Descartes included, go venal by teaching that the ability to think and the ability to think freely is the same thing. He applied his anatomical knowledge of the brain by identifying the habenula as the "seat of the soul, the source of FW." In modern times, Benjamin Libet, a physiologist with the University of California at San Francisco, as reported in a collection of articles from *Science News* in June, 2016, said this about FW: "The conscious mind does not initiate voluntary actions. I propose that the performance of every conscious voluntary action is preceded by special unconscious cerebral processes that begin about a one half second or so before the act." However, he does not rule out the existence of FW because further research might give it credibility.

Most animals do not have the ability to think and reason with the exception of those in the higher group of apes and to the bewilderment of science, crows. A study I read years ago answered the question "What makes us fearful of snakes?" It was not intended to prove or disprove FW but nevertheless, it postulated the idea that primal fear is so deeply ingrained in us that, being exposed to the proximity of snakes, we jump before we are consciously aware that we jump. Anytime we do something unconsciously, FW is left out in the cold. Study after study is proving that genes trump FW and the genetic disposition of behavior caused by genes is ignored by FW believers. These studies would make Calvin, Luther, and dozens of warriors of the faith proud to know that their beloved bondage of the will faith is beginning to show itself to others outside the church community. FW theology fabricates the power and viability of FW by assigning to it square hole characteristics that are designed to fit into round holes. FW theology as well as most people ignore the ramifications of studies showing how behavior, at any early age, is affected by genes. Are some people born criminals? In the 1970s, research conducted by neuroscientists was designed to measure if brain development was developing normally in 1795 three-year-olds. The children were hooked up to a polygraph to measure their reactions to a series of twelve tones beginning with pleasant sounds and ending with other high pitched and jarring sounds that were not pleasant. The part of the brain, the amygdala, is proven to be involved in processing fear. Twenty years later, court records were scoured to see whether any of the 1794 children had committed crimes involving violence, drugs, or serious driving offenses, and found that 137 had criminal records. Researchers than looked at the polygraph records of these 137 and every single one revealed that he/she did not register any different reactions between the pleasant and high pitched unpleasant sounds. These 137 could not tell the difference between a tone that should have elicited fear

> "Knowing yourself is the beginning of wisdom."
> ARISTOTLE

and one that should have elicited contentment. Fear of the other 1658 polygraph results showed a normal and recognizable differentiation. None of these had a criminal recod. Nothing was said about a possible hearing loss but I assume that this was ruled out. The conclusion arrived at: "If they were not afraid that their criminal behavior will land them in jail, what else will deter them?" The consensus was some people exhibit criminal behavior due to lack of conscious. This brings metaphysics (question of what is real and what is thought to be real) into play when FW believers think that our behavior is a result of FW. Philosophical metaphysics, unlike the field of physics which requires the use of the scientific method, does not require hard and fixed determinants to separate what is real from alternate realisms. An example would be artificial intelligence. Can a robot be just as intelligent as a human? Possibly, if the definition of IQ is changed. A better example would be religious or Bible metaphysics. The Bible says "All things are possible with God."(Matt. 19:26) The real thing here is some things are not possible with man but this real thing is changed to an alternative truth, resulting in two truths that are not contradictory. Philippians 4:13 tells us "I can do all things through Him who strengthens me." Looking outside the Bible at secular metaphysics, what is real? If I think I am attractive, am I attractive? If I think I am healthy, am I? Yes, I would be healthier than if I didn't think so. In my mind, can I accomplish mind over matter? No, not in my conscious mind, but science is becoming more certain that our unconscious mind can marshal more force and will than previously thought. Einstein said an atom won't move unless something moves it. I can extrapolate his meaning to say that he meant it can't move itself. Calvinists can use this principle to prove that a person can't cause himself to move a chair without help from outside his environmental space, so to speak. The energy required to lift something comes from food. FW can't be supported by the fact that when food is digested, the resulting energy belongs to the person who digested the food but this energy must be stimulated or activated. Even though the stimulus required to lift something seems to come from the lifter, it actually comes from something extraneous to the lifter. There must be a cause to lift a chair. In discussing cause and effect, the word "reason" can be used instead of "cause". My science books tell me that everything in this universe must have a reason (cause) to do what it does, a reason to create (cause) an effect. Darwin eliminated FW as a causative agent in his theory. Nothing happens at random unless a cause supersedes it. Yet as Darwin's Theory of Evolution spread throughout the world, in the many books I have read on this, not one of them questioned or even mentioned the possibility that FW is defunct. The shark evolved with many teeth because its evolution caused its teeth. When explained in these terms, FWers can't accept the fact that a person cannot claim FW credit for something as simple as moving a chair. But you can't give me one reason a person would have to move a chair that originates in that

> *"Every man is guilty of all the good he did not do."*
> VOLTAIR

person. If his leg itched, he would scratch his leg. If the sun was in his eyes, it wasn't FW that caused him to more it. FWers teach that their island is a secluded world unto itself but Calvinism and science teach that there is no such thing as an island that can barricade itself against worldly influences. A person is an integral part of the world evolving around him.

FW is arguably the key foundation piece that supports the theological tenets of the majority of Christian churches. But there are few people who would agree with that. The majority of theologians write books about atonement, the dual role of Jesus' divine versus human role, The Trinity, etc. An attempt to use FW as the foundation piece has not been made but I claim that FW has sufficient tentacles to grasp and embrace the major doctrines and link them together in a common platform. FW denies that salvation is secure. (Although some do teach it is). Pure FW holds that it can be

> *"Unconscious habits shape our souls."*
> T. S. ELLIOT

lost the same way it was obtained, by choosing. FW also denies total depravity at birth by claiming that some goodness was retained after the Fall. (Although some do teach total depravity) Lastly, FW theology teaches that Christ died for everyone and for those who do not choose Him, His death was not in vain because they were given the FW chance to choose Him. (Almost all teach this). The most dominant Christian denomination is The Catholic Church. The runner up is The Southern Baptist Church. The Presbyterian Church follows. Although it claims the Calvinist doctrine, it is in name only and does not actively teach its precepts. On down the list is the Lutheran Church and contrary to its name, does not have much in common with its namesake, Martin Luther. The majority, if not all, these churches teach FW. Near the bottom of a long list are the Reformed Churches and Calvinistic denominations that do teach the teaching of John Calvin and Martin Luther.

CAUSE AND EFFECT

Using the scientific principle of cause and effect with supporting scripture proves the invalidity of FW. However, the Bible is not needed to prove this. Theologians claim that FW is a biblical concept and have segregated it into an esoteric tool for doctrinal use. But FW is not biblical after the Adamic Fall. Scientists are invading this so-called FW territory and putting the field of will into its rightful place, science, where it can be studied and proven or disproven. It doesn't belong in the Bible because it doesn't exist. The Bible talks about the mind and body but science investigates their functions. Neuroscience is looking at fertile new-ground research in brain activity and the fields of psychology, and philosophy is joining in to look at the phenomenal things going on in human behavior. The Bible teaches that our wills are not free and until saved, we are in bondage to Satan and after salvation, bondage to Christ. The Book of Genesis tells us that God caused Adam to have as close to a FW as anyone ever had. The effect was Adam could do anything he wanted except eat from the Tree. There was no Commandments, law, or sin. Upon close reading, you will find that he was not even required to till his Garden. God gave him the Garden so he would have something pleasant to do. Sin would come later and with it, weeds and toil. Before the Fall, the absence of sin is what made Adam free. Later I will prove that sin eliminated FW. After the Fall, we are made free through the Blood of Christ and have a new kind of freedom that is better than the pre-Fall freedom that Adam had. God told him he was free to exercise dominion, which was not a requirement but rather a privilege. So, God was the "Causer" and Adam's FW was the effect. The principle of cause and effect is evidenced throughout the Bible. The force that some people call FW is not an intrinsic spontaneous process that is caused by a cognitive and deliberate act that originates in the conscious mind. It is not caused by our act, but rather by an act extraneous to our innate capability. After the brain finishes its processing, the results come to rest in the mysterious recesses of the mind. Some scientists maintain the brain and mind are one entity but as research grows, this belief is losing its provability. The absence of spontaneity is what prevents scientists from calling this intangible force FW. Since FWers insist that spontaneity must be present for FW to exist, they in effect have unknowingly trumped themselves out of business when science's jurisdiction took precedence over FW. And it is noticeable that at this point in their research, scientists are borrowing the term "free will" (saying it is not a valid term) from the religious sector. A simple principle of physics states that an atom or other object, in order to remain motionless or remain in motion, must have an accompanying cause to do so. An object in motion is not free to maintain that motion without the help of another force, gravity. But gravity is not the original cause that

> *"Insanity is a matter of degree."*
> JOAQUIM MARIA MACHADO DE ASSIS

causes an apple to fall. God invented gravity and He is the original cause and it's my job to emphasis the difference between primary and secondary causes. FW rests its case on secondary causes and is at a loss to explain the difference between primary and secondary but a secondary cause does not adequately explain why you went to the store and bought milk. Primary and secondary causes are used to explain what goes on in the complex makeup of our mind, brain, and body. The impetus of our behavior does not begin with a conscious freedom of thought, or with a spontaneous conscious thought originating within us. Coming to grips with cause and effect requires that we recognize what caused motion and behavior. This causes a halleluiah when we see that He was the primary cause when He said "Let there be light" and gives us an idea when motion replaced the void and gives us an appreciation for Einstein when he explained that light was mass. Einstein said that without motion, mass ceases to exist in its present state. Research is showing that we can actually see some of the particles that were first set in motion millions of years ago. FW can be examined under a hypothetical spiritual telescope when we apply Einstein's theory to see its correlation to FW. When FW was put in motion before Lucifer's fall, (he was the first to have FW) it ceased its existence, its motion if you will, in the post Fall Garden. Scientific research has been going on for years but prior to these latest findings, (which will be discussed later) I do not recall the use of FW in the scientific community. Science until recently has been reluctant to venture very far into the field of mind/brain research. That changed with the advent of gene mapping and brain imagining technology. But the mind-boggling research in the field of neuroscience is causing science to take a new look at things that until a few decades ago, were not even imagined. And this new look is bringing the correlation between science and religion closer than they have ever been, meaning science is beginning to see religion as new ground for exploration. This new look is prompted in part by the advent of MRI imaging and gene mapping. Science can now look into the hidden places like the subconscious mind. This is not to say that theology is accepting science's put down of FW. Science's new definition replaces FW with "will" and its use of FW in many scientific groups is in the negative. A simple description of the pathway that our driven will takes must start with a cause that prompts recognition by the brain, where electrical, chemical, and magnetic processes occur. Then the intangible mind does its part which activates the driven will, resulting in an effect, which is a decision or choice. Sometimes the effect is a decision, "I am going to marry her". Sometimes it's a physical action like closing a door.

In 2003, *The American College of Sports Medicine* reviewed ten studies dealing with the interaction of genes and physical activity. One study found that people's activity levels varied as much as 50% from one individual to another, depending on the individual's genetic code. Biologically and physiologically, this places genes in the driver's seat and throws FW out even as a passenger. This coding manifests itself in both physical and mental behavior and is divorced from any interference with or input from FW. The importance of this study

> *"Einstein did not speak a word until he was 6 or 7 years old."*

shows that genes affect not only our physical characteristics but also our decision making and behavior, as we will see in other studies. Barbara McClintock, a biologist, won the Nobel Prize in 1983 for her discovery that genes are not fixed links in the chain of a chromosome, proving the neural plasticity of the brain. Genes can roam around and alter their function. Our brain's neocortex, which is the largest of the two-part brain and which is responsible for regulating our conscious and probably unconscious behavior, has about 100 billion cells, each with 1,000 to 10,000 synapses, trillions of connections, and 300 million feet of "wiring". This roaming causes our behavior to change and influences us to make decisions based on factors we are not aware of and are blind to any alleged behavior caused by FW. Science has proven that our genes and environment at an early age shape our lifetime behavior and leave little room for pseudo behavior caused by FW. This shaping was proven decades ago and even then, before today's research, FW was nonchalantly claiming validity in the face of scientific fact. This shaping counterman's FW. The scientific community knew this for many years but it has only been the last few years that science has proven the huge impact of the role played by genes and environment in regards to both conscious and unconscious behavior.

Research now revolves around the mind/brain/gene/environment complex. Our brain is comprised of separate regions, each region regulating either vision, hearing, touch, balance, movement, emotional response, and any other function requiring a need for a decision. We are not consciously aware of why we make most of our decisions. I may think I know why I called my Mom. It was because I loved her. And I do. But the reason I love her is not of my own making. It was because she loved me. This was why I called her. She caused me to love her and therefore caused me to call her. We make the mistake of thinking we cause one another to love each other. This is an easy cause and effect example that disproves FW if we leave it as is. But what if I am able to make a case that she did not freely choose to love me. She was compelled to love me as all mothers are compelled to love their offspring. The situation of a drug addict or unbalanced mother is a different situation. This compulsion to love is God given, even to unsaved mothers. The difficulty in untangling the lies built with FW is these lies are tied together by the heartstrings of love and these heartstrings wrap up a love package erroneously attributed to coming from human origins. All things good come from God, not from FW, not from me, not from you, or from the trillions of mothers and dads. The love in us comes from God and emanates through us to those we love. This book is not about detracting from the power of love. Its focus is to zero in on ramifications of cause and effect and go blindly where it leads regardless of the many side trails (secondary causes) that pop up. Our love for one another is a secondary cause. Phillip Wiley wrote about mother's love more than sixty years ago in his book, "Generation of Vipers". He did not directly address FW or cause and effect. The book did not tell what his motive was but I suspect he was motivated by an unhappy childhood and a bad relationship with his mother. His accusation was that mothers used the mother-child relationship as a tool to control and manipulate their offspring and did not downplay the role of a mother's love but indicated that some mothers allow selfish motives to undermine the love motive. This proves to me that love, to some degree, can be replaced by our selfish motives. This lines up with science and the Bible. Both teach that the force of any trait can be overridden by a greater force. In effect, the force that Satan has over a lost person can be overridden by the blood of Jesus. Our will can be overridden by the will of Jesus, who lives in us. I am not qualified to discuss the difference between the Bible's "Love conquers all" and its teaching that God hated Ismael. I will leave this up to the Hebrew scholars who can give a correct interpretation of God's hate. I am qualified to discuss how God loved Adam and when Adam became spiritually dead, God did not love a spiritually dead Adam in the same manner as His love for the pre-Fall Adam, and when God hardened Pharaoh's heart (Exodus 10:1), this exemplifies the difference between the Bible's "God is love" nature and other scripture that teaches that God dispenses His love and mercy in a discretionary manner. This is contrary to the FW belief that God's mercy is available to anyone who exercises FW. The phrase "for God so loved the world" does not mean He

> *"I know, O Lord, that the way of man is not in himself; it is not in any man to walk and direct his steps."*
>
> *Jeremiah 10:23*

loves everyone in the world. Wiley's book did not make the best sellers list because of his caustic attack on Moms and apple pie. I would be in physical danger if I told a mother that her love for her child did not initially come from her. God, in His long suffering, accepts the belief in FW the same as His acceptance of our other sins. This is why FW will live until Christ comes back and is why Christian's will continue to sin, although hidden by the Blood, until we are fully redeemed. FW is simple and uncomplicated and like a mother's love, warms the cockerels of our hearts. It's noteworthy that Wiley got a jump on the scientific trend of today that lends credence to the belief that we are not what we seem to be or who we think we are. The Bible teaches that we are as rags in God's eyes without Christ's covering. Too many Christians think of themselves as worthy based partly on works and humanitarian good deeds and this at the expense of Christ's work in us. The reason FW cannot be disbelieved is we refuse to proclaim Christ as the total cause of everything good and we cannot give Him credit as the source for the totality and originator of our blessings. Paul was adamant in giving Christ total credit and did not use the term "cause and effect", but he, like the other Apostles, never claimed credit for any accomplishments. Christ is the cause of someone being able to help himself. The old adage that a man can pull himself up by his bootstraps does not give credit to the cause behind the pulling. When someone works hard every day, it is good and normal to want credit and recognition because we were designed to accomplish things and perform best when we are recognized and rewarded but God wants us to recognize Him as the cause of everything good. God gives us the ability to work and He wants us to recognize ourselves for the good works we do but self- recognition must take a back seat to God-recognition. Romans 8:28 tells us "and we know that <u>God causes all things to work together....</u>" God is the initial causer of all work even though He wants us to be recognized as helpers. The phenomenal meaning of this verse is sometimes overlooked. "All" means all. He takes wars and tornadoes and sin and makes them into something "good for those that love Him" This is a mystery beyond our understanding. An analogy can be made between our work for God and the work our children do for us. If the child carries out the trash, he should be rewarded even though we were the cause of him being able and having the opportunity to work. If there were no rewards for work, little work would be done, proven by Revelation 14:13. "...and their works do follow them". This tells me that God recognizes our work but we are prone to take too much credit for ourselves. Paul gives us the guide to follow. As a mature bond servant, his reward was his ability to serve Christ. As Christians mature, they should seek less recognition and model themselves accordingly. Babies want and need all the primary selfish recognition and devotion they can get but after training, they should become less dependent. There is no better example of selfish dependence than that of a child. 1 Corinthians 13:11 says "When I was a child I used to speak like a child, think like a child, reason like a child; when I became a man, I did away with childish things." We have to look in the Bible to know what causes a baby's selfishness (sin). In the New Testament, we are told that all are born into sin and in adulthood, we all, to varying degrees, retain our infancy. It's impossible to not sin because it's ingrained in us until, as Paul describes, we are fully redeemed. This is why it's hard to give up FW.

Modern day science is replacing science fiction of the past. The fictitious behavior in the movie "The Manchurian Candidate" is now fact. The Candidate was depicted as a human robot void of FW and controlled by an outside force. Although this statement will not be accepted by the FW community, we are robots who are controlled by forces that, in 95 percent of life events, we are not aware of. Science has proven that mind control is fact, not fiction, by way of hypnosis and subliminal suggestion and research showing the subconscious brain as the mastermind of our behavior. And we know the subconscious brain acts in accordance with genetic disposition and environment. In recent years, mind/brain research has expanded but FW believers continue to believe the myth of freedom. Science fiction has become science. The movie was enjoyed for its science fiction motif and though exaggerated, it supports the scientific view that our choices do not come from where we think they do.

> *"A good speech is like a pencil. It has to have a point and eraser."*
> — SAM SHIPLEY

Bill Clinton said that when gene mapping was completed, it was the greatest scientific achievement in two centuries. Our brains are formed and shaped by genes and environment. We know that behavior is determined by the chemical, electrical, and magnetic activities taking place in the neurons and synapses of the brain. A neuron fires each time we think a thought, smell an odor, see danger, experience a hug, or experience tens of thousands of other external environmental stimuli, and this is in addition to the internal stimulus occurring in our conscious and subconscious minds. FW is so phony it can't even be classified as a hypothesis. Our awareness state of mind is very limited because our conscious faculty has a limited amount of storage space. We marvel at a young mind that we say can absorb things like a sponge but this is because a baby doesn't have much information and don't need much storage space. As the child gets older, the sponge begins to become rigid. There is a gene that causes a neurochemical release that promotes happiness. Like all genetic processes, these happy genes cannot be turned off or on without the help of a stimulus that originates outside our sphere of control. I was born with a happy gene but not born with the ability to turn it on or off by conjuring up, without stimulus, thoughts of being happy. Even if we attempt to fake a happy thought to get a genuine happy feeling, this cannot be attributed to FW because we would have to rely on

> "Imagination and fiction make up more than three quarters of our real life." Simon Well, a 1909–1943 French philosopher. Its more than amazing that he said then what modern day science is saying now."

a happy event stored in our memory and this would entail borrowing from an event that we did not cause from within ourselves. Using a baby is a good way to explain this. If you tickle the baby, it becomes happy and grins. You will not see a baby tickle itself and grin by way of spontaneity. You will not see an adult become happy unless he has a reason to be happy. Happiness does not come from within unless you are a Hindu and believe that happiness cannot be found in the world, or anywhere else, and resides in the person. A Christian can't conjure up happiness from within himself because Philippians 4:7 tells us "...

peace of God, which surpasses all comprehension ..." I believe that peace is a derivative of happiness and I acknowledge a person could propel himself into a happy state through meditation but this is a learned process and will not work without the help of an outside higher power and this cannot be credited to FW. When peace is accomplished through meditation, it's reasonable to say that peace is good even thought it was not attained through prayer (I can't think of a bad peace). Since all good things come from God, it did not come from FW. We were born with a happy gene but not born with a reason to be happy. There is no trigger to automatically activate that gene. The reason is we were born into sin and there is nothing happy about sin except in the short term. All newborns come out of the womb crying and will continue until they are caused to be happy. We were born with a gene that is dormant and waiting for God, a parent, or friend to be the instrument or trigger for the release of a neurochemical. All newborns are under stress, which causes the release of cortisol. If we were born without stress, without the stress gene, we would be born happy and remain in a continuous state of happiness. It would not be any fun or enjoyable to stay happy. I am thankful for my childhood and teen years of poverty because it makes me thankful for my austere comfort as an adult. Staying happy would also negate God's design which is, when stimulated, a chemical is released which results in a happy chemical stimulating a happy gene thus causing happiness. If it was intended for us to be born happy and stay happy, He would have placed this chemical as a constant substance in our blood. A Christian, or anyone else for that matter, cannot feel free or feel real happiness without God's intervention. It can't be mustered up through FW.

I am plagiaristic in the sense that I did not come to the above conclusions without help from others. Everything in this book has, in one way or the other, been borrowed from others. This borrowing has been tempered with my own perspective but this uniqueness does not support the idea that I came to these conclusions without help from external causes. I use Martin Luther as an example. Before I read his "Bondage of the Will" and the supporting scripture, I had no idea how ludicrous FW is. He, Calvin, and others planted the germ and it grew into this book. In this sense, we are all plagiarists, and like babies, were born without any knowledge of the outside world yet we are taught early on that we can do anything by exercising FW without being influenced by outside sources. The contradiction posed by FW is this belief acknowledges exposure to outside sources but denies this exposure is sufficient to cause us to act or choose. But contrary to this teaching, we just keep growing and knowing and feeding on the sources around us. As far as information dissemination, we started as new babes and ended as old babes. The point is we don't have FW as a new babe or grow into it as we age. A baby is a perfect example of the nonsense of FW. Everything a baby does is caused by a source that is outside its scope of control. Solomon tells us there is nothing new under the sun. There is nothing new about the belief in FW. It has survived for centuries. Desires, hopes, and aspirations of our modern world are not new, just wrapped in modern world clothing. Freedom has always been a primary goal, freedom from hunger, oppression, fear and loneliness. FW has been a perfect scam to meet this goal. The point that is hard to make and harder to accept is FW is not the mechanism for accomplishing these goals. FW does not accomplish anything and is just a trash barrel for storing problems that don't have a handy solution. That is to say it's hard to identify what causes some behavior or events and rather than take the time to logically analyze its genesis, it's easy and convenient to label FW as the cause. The definition of plagiarism (borrowing or stealing someone's idea), when applied to theology, can be used to show how illegal FW is. FW teaches that an idea or cause can *originate* from within ourselves. One example is the Bible teaches that the Holy Spirit is our helper. In the case of someone who has not been saved yet, that person does not have the Holy Spirit in him but FW teaches that a person can be saved by the power that is in that person.

The principle of primary cause and effect as defined in this book must be the determining factor in who the primary owner is. The problem is sometimes claims are based on our secondary involvement. The dictionary definition places as much importance on secondary causes as it does on primary (first) causes by limiting itself to short term theft or illegal copying but the accurate definition would place more emphasis on a primary cause, thus making it compatible with the scientific principle of cause and effect as used in this book. Can an idea, event, or property be traced to its original primary cause? A row of dominos standing end to end and falling sequentially can be brought down by tripping the first domino. We are all plagiarists in anything we write, think, or speak because everything we do is based on someone else's thoughts and efforts. This radical statement will not fit well even with Calvinists. To say otherwise would be like claiming the ability to make new matter. That long tunnel in Switzerland is being used in an attempt to find a particle smaller than anything we know of but if they do find it, it will not be a new creation. Matter can't be destroyed or created. God caused universal matter and He will destroy it when

> *"Some days you are the dog.*
> *Some days the hydrant."*
> TOM T. HALL

He creates a new Heaven and Earth. An oxygen molecule traveling through our lungs will either be modified if used, or unchanged if an excess amount is present. In either case, it can't be destroyed. An article discussing theoretical physics explained that a molecule that came from someone's lungs thousands of years ago is still floating around in the atmosphere today. This is not an exaggeration. The article said the molecule is still here. An example of this unbelievable phenomenon (matter can't be destroyed) can be allegorically used in discussing a new idea but there is no such thing as a new idea if consideration is given to the fact that most ideas are a composite whole consisting of sub-parts that have been previously known and publicized. Einstein's Theory of Relativity is new only in the sense that he was the first to borrow (plagiarize if you will) ideas from others in order to make a composite whole. I don't believe this composite whole should be described as original but certainly the author should be credited with joining something old to make something new. After a jigsaw puzzle has been finished, can it be said that the finished puzzle is original, or would it be fairer to say the whole can't be original but each part's originality combines to make a whole consisting of individual original parts. We are individually unique in regards to genetic makeup, biological composition, and soul/spirit but there is nothing unique in regards to our thoughts and behavior. Solomon said there is nothing new under the sun. I can't be positive, but I think he was referring to the human experience of behavior, thought, and deeds. I believe that no matter how hard we try to be unique, there will be something in our behavior or accomplishments that was borrowed from a non-self source. The discoverer of insulin learned from his anatomy teachers that the pancreas was where insulin was produced and from his chemistry teachers the cellular interaction of glucose. Without this knowledge, he would not have discovered insulin. This discovery, like many others, was a joint venture and what caused its discovery should be attributed to everyone who played a part. I believe his teachers should share some of the discovery credit and in this sense, plagiarism was required in the discovery process. I agree this is a strict interpretation of plagiarism that would not withstand a legal challenge. The person who discovered insulin did not discover anatomy and chemistry and these discoveries provided the foundation on which the discovery of insulin was based. One man cannot be the sole originator of anything. It takes a village. Originality, when confined to a strict definition, and FW, are non-existent. The discovery of thousands of medical products as well as scientific discoveries such as electricity and steam engines cannot be attributed to the originality of one man. The point to be made is FW is not free but must be harnessed into servitude and bondage, which is either bondage to sin or bondage to Christ. I acknowledge that when a quilt is pieced together, its composite total is unique but when using the steps required to make a quilt, which were not acquired from self, the hard and fast rule of primary cause and effect requires me to give credit to the many people who taught someone the individual steps. I don't believe that a person who was not exposed to any fabric construction could wake up some day and make a quilt. In this sense, I believe a quilt maker commits acceptable plagiarism when viewed in a strict esoteric manner. The construction of Solomon's Temple was not one man's original, unique, or sole idea when considering the step by step construction that had to be learned. The workers had to learn how to make large stones. Knowledge had to be gained how to get these large boulders up hundreds of feet. He plagiarized and used everything around him. In using plagiarism in this sense, it is simply another way of proving that environment causes behavior and FW plays no part. When Adam was created he had a perfect environment and his FW created a perfect relationship with God. I borrow the theme from Hilary Clinton's book *It Takes a Village.* Our global village now has such a cohesive dependence that I can talk with anyone in the most outer reaches almost instantly in areas with cell phone towers and this global reach causes our behavior to be globally plagiaristic. Our global environment now causes our behavior to change from a provincial to a global dynamic. My behavior (even if I don't send money) is now caused by a starving child in Kenya as well as a child who goes to school hungry in my neighborhood village. Clinton's "Village" theme helps a non-FW believer to see the correlation between behavior and environment. FWers believe they are shaped by FW but the undeniable fact is we are shaped by environment. The world, like people, is too small to be shielded from change. Its behavior and ours must adapt to these changes.

We can't claim first title to anything but are only the holder of the second mortgage in terms of both thought and deed. As a side note, but germane to God's sovereignty, I relate one of the most consoling treasures I own. I am only just a speck or grain of sand, not only in the universe but in the vast knowledge of God's imminent domain. I try to keep this idea foremost in my mind in dealing with big problems by reducing them to a small scale when compared to the vastness of God's world in order to place them in their proper perspective. This keeps me grounded as to Who the original owner is and Who was the primary causer. In regards to plagiarism, I am reminded of a lawsuit in which someone was sued because of a copyright infringement. The winner of the lawsuit won because he was able to trace the cause of his ownership rights back several generations of his forefathers. I have never had an original thought in my life. Everything I am is based on and caused by someone or something in my past. I insert a disclaimer that I am not infallible, which you already knew, and hope that admitting my fallibility will not be mistaken for an attempt at modesty. I have never read a book in which the author acknowledges fallibility or that he could be wrong in at least something. My confession of fallibility longs for company and I just wish more authors would be this honest. Many of the claims and ideas in this book have been lying dormant in my subconscious mind until something causes them to appear in my conscious mind that for years had been stored in my mind's bookshelf waiting for a cause or reason to appear.

I base this claim on scientific research regarding the subconscious mind and its awesome ability to retain long forgotten information.

The most heart wrenching tragedy outside of a war zone was one I saw on a documentary TV show many years ago. It was about a South American poverty- stricken country that hosted many American tourists. There were many children roaming the streets, asking for handouts and sometimes stealing them and running. These children were homeless, dirty, and hungry. They were orphans whose families kicked them out and the state had no money to provide orphanages or give the kids any help. They were on their own and lived in the only safe place in the city, the underground sewers where no one else wanted to go. The kids became

> *"The conscious acts like a lid, taking things out and putting things in the unconscious*
> SIGMUND FREUD

uncontrollable and the police were given the order to shoot them like rats. They were called Rat Kids. The narrator of the show was wearing a hidden mike and the sound of police shooting was recorded but no actual shootings were recorded. The reporter went underground in the sewer pipes to interview the kids. What brought it to this point was tourism began to decline because of the Rat Kids and the city economy was suffering. The decision was made that something had to be done. This inhuman tragedy does more to prove the nonsense of FW as a plausible force than a scientific project focused on subconscious decision making. This story has a human element and the scientific projects addressed in this book do not reflect the utter inhumanity of shots being fired and kids forced to live in sewers. Without help from God, how can these kids use their FW to get more food, clean clothes, love, or anything else? How can anything good be attributable to FW? How can these kids' FW enable them to influence the government to help them? Keep in mind that if anything good or positive comes from outside that sewer to help these kids, in order for you to be honest, you would have to change your mind about the efficacy of FW because a FW believer is unrelenting in his demand that FW is a force within us, without any outside influence, that enables us to do something entirely on our own. These kids were on their own and starving and did not have the FW ability to help themselves. This happened many years ago and surely has not been allowed to continue.

A few years ago, TV's Sixty Minutes did a documentary on a village called Medimein in Columbia. Because of intermarriage and remoteness, every person in that village had a mutated gene that caused them to die from Alzheimer's Disease at about the age of fifty-five or younger. This was documented in a 1997 report in The AMA Journal. This is known as Mendel's Law, (The Father of Genetics) which shows that reproductive genes follow a predictable law that controls our hereditary traits passed from generation to generation These Medimein villagers are in primary bondage to their tradition of intermarriage. This primary bondage, in turn, caused a gene mutation which in turn caused their disease. This is an example of

> *"Discontent is the mother of creativity because nothing of value ever came from a contented person."*
> SAM SHIPLEY

multiple causation. Almost everything has multiple causes. On a small scale, this village is representative of a larger group, the human race. We are in primary bondage to our disobedience to God, which in turn caused sin, followed by our loss of FW. When Martin Luther and John Calvin established Calvinism, bondage (the opposite of FW) was the most important aspect of Calvinism, in my opinion. Today the term environment is used more often than bondage. We are in bondage to either our environment or genes or a combination of the two. Our environment (or genes) is our bondage. Today's Calvinism as taught by theologians is picking up on the new discoveries of the mind/brain complex but the laity has not been exposed to any degree but the theologians have not yet come into the full spotlight of science. Changing culture changes the way we behave. A documentary aired on TV on 20-20 in May, 1917, did a good job of discussing behavior caused by being addicted to phone texting, watching too much TV, video games, and other digital device usage. Brain scans showed the adverse effects on the brain that can't be reversed. This shows how the changing dynamics of our brain change the dynamics of our behavior. Yet society still relies on FW as the cause of most behavior. Environment has dealt us another blow in sneaking in and causing our longevity to drop as much as twenty years in some parts of the U.S., according to a recent 2017 study published in the JAMA. Researchers conclude this longevity drop may be caused by poverty. The highest drops were in Kentucky, Appalachia, the Mississippi Delta, and the Dakotas. Poverty's impact is on the younger age group. These youngsters cannot freely choose a more prosperous life on their own without help from outside sources. In order to correctly assess this, poverty should not be labeled as the primary cause of their shortened life span. To find the primary cause(s), we have to identify what caused the poverty. Maybe the coal mines closed down. FW will not help these kids or their families. They could move and this could solve the problem but this could not be attributed to FW. A move would require a new job. A new job would require a better economy. A better economy would require factories to increase their production. These things are outside influences that can change their situation, not FW. The most important consideration in studying environment is regardless of what happens in the children's lives after having been exposed to poverty, their adult lives will forever be shaped by not having enough to eat, going without TV, wearing second hand clothes, not having enough money to go to the prom, or having to stay home and the other kids going to a movie. This shaping cannot be altered by FW. I have experienced this first hand and see the correlation between my childhood poverty and my adult decisions and behavior. I know there are millions who have been raised in poverty and have not connected the dots and believe in FW because it is such a dominant force. This erroneous belief will cause us to think that FW is what causes our choice of church, neighborhood, and other social aspects. What is a constant amazement to me is FWers may acknowledge that in some cases, FW does not apply. They pick and choose and apply the power of FW as the causative agent for choosing how many children they have and deny that the cause was environment or genes. At the same time, they may agree that their child joined the military because it's a family tradition

> *Believing in FW while a child is in itself an environmental shaper that will have a behavioral impact that will be hard to shake.*

for four generations. These are examples drawn from first-hand experience in talking to friends or family. I could drop the entire issue of FW if people could see that they use logic (which is actually cause and effect) to solve some problems, like buying a truck instead of a car. Professor Indre Viskontas, in her *Course Guidebook*, says "We tend to think that rationality is what drives our big decisions-that we only make an important decision after carefully evaluating our options and weighing all the pros and cons. But the relatively new science of behavioral economics, coupled with decades of psychology research, is poking fairly large holes in this myth. The truth is that we are not only largely irrational in how we decide, but predictably so." Some people I have talked to don't have a problem in crediting logic as a cause yet still believe their choices are FW choices. This does not make sense because logic and FW are diametrically opposed. Logic works because it uses observations from all sources around us. FW allegedly works because it is based on inward observations that are not influenced or fettered by anything in the environment. FW is anchored in emotion and when I say I love my son because he is my son, this emotional declaration ignores fact, logic, and the Bible. The primary reason (logic) I love my son is "We love because He first loved us." 1 John 4:19. This translates: I could not love my son or anyone else if God had not first loved me. My claim applies to both the saved and unsaved. God poured His love out on humanity. Love conquers all and crosses all boundaries. Viskontas adds another insight into our irrational decision-making. She states it's a myth that we make rational decisions because "Most of our thoughts are dominated by self-talk, and our conscious mind is not privy to many of the processes that lead to our decisions". There is no room for FW here because even FWer's teach that behavior must be consciously caused in order for it to be a FW event.

In a poor neighborhood like Chicago or Kentucky, a child or family can rise above their poor environment and supposedly, without any outside help, improve their lives and as they look back, they will claim they did it on their own. The hardest thing for me, and I guess for others, was connecting the dots between genes, environment, and God. I believe that most people who read this will say that I have trashed hard work as the American way of getting ahead. But to be clear, I am saying that the god of FW is not what makes a better life on earth or a place in Heaven. God, genes, and environment are the tools of trade that allow us to get ahead. Hard word plays a part but when we ignore the primary reason that caused us to work hard, we short change the real and primary cause. We learned it from our parents or from wanting what the neighbors have. Some people use FW as a pick and choose FW when they say it applies in some situations but not others. In using it this way, it changes its definition each time a new circumstance arises. By now, you will see that I am attacking FW like a chicken after a bug but I see how FW has permeated our culture so deeply that it will never be changed. This is a worldwide belief and I can understand why it is treated like a god. I claim it is the glue that holds denominations together. Understanding the truth of the matter would not require us to change our lifestyle. Believing, as science proves, that our subconscious is the behavioral cause, would not require anything different than what we do now. Believing that we are not as smart as we think might bruise our ego but what we would get in return would be worth the price. Giving more credit and praise to God would be a cheap price for what we would get in return. Those who believe in FW have to be blind to the role that genes play but if they agree that FW does not have a hand in genetics but operates freely in other biological and psychological areas, they believe that FW has a dual role. This is a contradictory role because they would be agreeing that FW cannot control a gene that controls heredity but can control a gene that controls behavior, possibly like a happy gene. Studies support the belief that a child raised in a loving home will pay this love forward and a child raised in a Muslim country will remain Muslim (unless an outside influence like God intervenes). Believing that we do things altruistically takes the fun out of it when we accept the hard to accept belief that there are ulterior motives that we do not want to accept. Bill Gates said he gave away millions because he did not want the third world children to drink contaminated water. Was this the primary reason? Luther would say Gates was bound to give, bound by something he was not aware of. When we give something, we sometimes do not know if it is a good cause. Romans 8:28 has given me freedom from any concern that it may not be worthy. "All things work together for the good for those who love God". This verse keeps us out of trouble when doubt arises concerning giving and is the strongest anchor in the Bible when highlighting "All things". If you make a mistake and give it to the wrong charity, God will make it work to the good. I am not saying we can do anything we want and God will make it right. I am saying that if our heart is in the right place, a wrong decision will work to the good. This verse was a lifesaver when I decided to move to Florida fourteen years ago. We sold everything we had, left all our friends and relatives, and moved to a place that at first I did not like at all. We left a place I loved and I worried that we made the wrong move. I began to love God with "all my heart, soul, and mind". Sure enough, things began to fall in place. Events happened that convinced me I was where God wanted me to be. It's difficult to describe this feeling but the security and peace, as one scripture says, that surpasses all understanding, is priceless. I mined Romans 8:28 and found a nugget I was not expecting. "All things" should be interpreted as inclusive. There is nothing that can escape God's remedial fixing, even sin. If I make a mistake and love God, He will make it alright. I go a step further to say that when I sin, repent, and love God, His forgiveness represents something good and therefore it "works together for the good." After all, He forgave me of my sins and saved me and this is a perfect example of turning my sin into something good. After salvation, He keeps forgiving me, thus turning my continual sin into something good. The results of sin are death but Jesus died for me. My counsel to those who feel they are not in the right place, whether it be in marriage, job, or abode, is to tell God you are tired of being stressful and doubtful and ask Him where He wants you. "Those who wait upon the Lord will renew their strength". This is not an easy thing to do until you make a habit of it. Only by waiting can you become stronger. So many of our blessings take time. Time is what strengthens our faith. If God gave us

> "I want to be buried face down because everything in this world is upside down. When I am fully redeemed and the world is set straight back up, I will be looking in the right direction again."
>
> PARAPHRASED FROM A FORGOTTEN PHILOSOPHER

what we asked for instantly, there would be no need for faith. It takes waiting to see the "evidence of things hoped for." Waiting can be construed as a form of work. When we wait, we get stronger. The only way to make a straited muscle stronger is to work it. FW cannot make all things work together because FW is dictated by self. Verse 28 is dictated by God. Gates may or may not acknowledge God in his giving but if he does, he probably does not believe that God caused him to make billions so he could help the children. It's possible that Gates believed that God allowed him to make billions and then left it up to Gate's FW as to how to use the money. I am not saying he was not concerned about the children's welfare. Throughout this FW narrative, I am attempting to make it clear that our behavior and decisions are the result of primary causes which we are not aware of and by secondary causes we are aware of. People may think the million things that have happened to them since birth are stored in a convenient pull out drawer and can be consciously accessed to be used in conscious decision making. This is said in reference to the million things that pertain to our environmental upbringing. But we don't have FW control of our environment or FW control of our upbringing. In addition, we don't have control of our genetic inheritance. People with high IQs have an innate ability, one that cannot be freely and consciously activated, to make high test score. If our actions are not conscious, they are not FW. This ability is genetically driven. The idea that we are self-made men whose entrepreneurship is the primary factor that gets us ahead in life is deeply imbedded in our capitalistic American culture. The axiom that "God helps those who help themselves" is clearly intended to mean that we must first help ourselves and God follows and gives His help. But the problem with this statement is we can't do anything good unless God takes the lead. As a bondage believing person, I claim that God is the Initiator, Originator, Determinator, and Sovereign Dispenser of blessings that are totally conditioned and caused by His grace and His grace alone. Any time we claim anything good as coming from us <u>first</u> is a theology tantamount to bordering on atheism. But remarkably, God, through His long suffering, "suffers" Christians to believe otherwise. The Bible teaches that nothing good can **originate** from either an unsaved or saved person. It teaches that a saved person is empowered by God to do good things.

A good environment is one of the reasons that causes children to be more successful in later life. Our changing culture is not given enough credit in the way it changes our behavior. A study published in the *Science News Magazine* dated 8-5-17 and conducted by Psychologist Bettina Lamon and colleagues of Osnabruck University in Germany shows the environmental impact on early childhood development. It offers no encouragement to the existence of FW. The study compared the self-control of a group of four-year-old Cameroon youngsters with that of a group of four-year-olds from Germany. The children were given a marshmallow and told they could eat it now and not get another one or wait and get a second one in addition to the first. 70 percent of the Cameroon kids waited ten minutes before eating and received the second treat. Only 28 percent of the German children waited in order to get a second treat. The parenting practices of the Cameroon kids throughout childhood consisted of more supervisory control like Moms taking the lead in organizing play activities and limiting the kid's ability to make decisions in regards to game rule interpretation. A child was taught to keep his emotions in check and emphasis was placed on respecting elders. The parenting practices of the German kids reflected the Western culture of emphasizing independence and allowing expressions of how they feel and what they want. Psychologists in the study concluded that a child who is raised in a Western culture is taught that he can get what he wants when he wants it and to have to wait for it creates a sense of loss of control. This study supports the idea that children should be taught how to deal with a feeling of loss of control rather than how to prevent those feelings from occurring. Follow up studies of Western and non-Western children seem to show that the children who waited in order to get another treat were more successful and had academic and social advantages decades later.

> *"It's not hard to meet new expenses, they are everywhere. But new friends are a different matter."*
> — SAM SHIPLEY

Britton Chance of the University of Pennsylvania is a biophysicist who worked in lie detector technology in 2003. His research concentrated on the brain's pre-frontal cortex, where lies are born. Volunteers were asked to answer some questions truthfully and lie about others. The researchers knew the volunteer was going to lie before the conscious decision to lie was made. The blood flow imagining signaled the decision to lie before the volunteer consciously knew he was going to lie. His unconscious mind made the decision before his conscious mind decided to lie. The blood flow spike showed the unconscious decision to lie came before the conscious decision to lie was made. This proves that the subconscious mind is the only thing that has FW (I say this in humor) and serves as the shepherd for herding things in and out of the conscious mind. Although

> "Reality consists of two different substances, material and thinking."
> RENE DESCARTES

not a part of the study, this tells us where unconscious decisions may also be formed or created. And there may not be a dichotomy between the realms of conscious and unconscious decision making. This is my opinion based on the blood flow that showed up in the region of the brain that houses the autonomic nervous system reflexes, which are involuntary. If I understand it right, the researchers identified the part of the brain where sublime and involuntary reactions live, and maybe along-side our other reactions, which are voluntary? So it appears the voluntary and involuntary reactions reside in the same region but being housed together does not mean they share the same role or function. Our wills are fragile and promiscuous as anyone can attest because on any day anything can go wrong with our conscious decision making and we many times don't know why. Everyone has a will. No one has a FW. There is no difference between a saved and unsaved person's will in regards to the will's instability in regards to non-salvation issues. However, as a Christian, I have the will of Christ in me and will have the will to sin until, as Paul tells us, we are fully redeemed. A Christian can make as many bad decisions as a lost person in regards to non-salvation issues but in regards to salvation, it is impossible for someone who has been chosen (and later saved) before the foundation to make a bad choice. This is because Calvinistic theology and the Bible teach that God's choice of salvation cannot be rescinded by the one chosen.

Salvation does not insure the stability of the will. Science defines our will based on our mind's duality. Our subconscious mind has a will that mostly overrides our conscious will. According to the FW believer's own definition of FW, an unconscious decision cannot be a FW decision. Other research has pinpointed the location of conscious activity.

In gene mapping, the goal was to determine the assignment and function of each gene. This was followed by more mapping of the brain to find out more detail about some regions of the brain that remain in question. The hardest research seems to be over. Attention can now be focused on genome editing. This editing is similar to editing done in a word processor. An article in this book contains a quote from a neurologist who said that of the millions of things we do or think, every one of them is marked by a gene. After the assignments were finalized, more mapping of the brain to find out more detail about some regions of the brain that remain in question were completed. Genes can be turned on or off, repaired, and modified to eliminate undesirable inherited traits. The point is genes can be altered, giving us another avenue to examine unlearned

> *"A low sodium intake has been shown to stimulate the sympathetic nervous system which may be associated with increased cardiovascular disease."*
> FRANK MESSERLI, M.D.
> (I WISH THEY COULD MAKE UP THEIR MINDS)

behavior, and behavior that is genetically controlled that circumvents the control of our will. Every alteration will reflect a behavioral alternation. Gene mapping alone is enough to prove FW is not viable by showing the link between behavior and the subconscious mind. The January 2018 magazine *Science News* had an article explaining that gene-editing technology regarding a baby's genes has developed to the point that inherited diseases like diabetes and obesity can be eliminated by altering a certain gene that was discovered with gene mapping. As this technology improves, there is hardly no limit to the improvement in health caused by gene modification. Genes are responsible for passing on hereditary traits and the ones that control our happiness and joys have been marked. Sexual activity and eating rank (mine is pizza) among the top physical activities we enjoy because they promote happiness and this is a fact but I say in jest that if we could use FW to curtail our happy gene while eating, FW would replace the Mediterranean diet and tummy tucks. Hinduism teaches that the way to escape delusion and disappointment is to cease searching for happiness from without, from the world, and find it from within. Hinduism then would be more pro-FW than Christianity. Hindus know the danger of the happy gene. This teaching lines up with Christianity that teaches us to avoid seeking worldly happiness at the expense of that which is found in the Kingdom but the Hindu practice of seeking happiness from within is not a "Christ in me" source. The Hindu practice aliens itself with FW because it teaches ignoring environmental factors that come from outside.

A happy gene that is successful in creating happiness is self-propagating and self-rewarding by passing on its ability to succeed to its next generation. This mimics Darwin's Theory of Evolution in which survival of the fittest favors gene longevity. This is the happy news but for most people, those who don't have time to sit around and philosophize, the sad news is that too much of a happy thing is sad. Philippians 3:19 tells us "...whose god is their appetite ..." This and many more scriptures tell us the folly of FW. Habakkuk 2:5 tells us "...he enlarges his appetite like Sheol, and he is like death, never satisfied...." Overeating, to a much lesser degree, is like alcoholism or any other addition. It can be controlled with outside help but the genetic predisposition is untouchable. Our autonomic nervous system kicks in to either help or hurt the abuses we create. We can't control our hunger but can control the degree of hunger by drinking water or using other techniques that trick or program our thinking. When sugar was first discovered and found that it enhances our taste buds, someone added more sugar to get more enhancement (happiness). White flower and sugar have caused so much happiness that they are killing us. The more sugar we eat the more we want. Stated in another way but just as true, the more happiness we get the more we want. Happiness is the most contagious good emotion we have but also the most contagious disease when our food intake is abused. Sugar is emblematic of our eating culture. The more we eat the more we want. Solomon said "All human toil is for the mouth, and yet the appetite is not satisfied." (Ecclesiastes 6:7) Nutrition informs us that if we ate only what our body needs, we could approach the longevity of our ancient forefathers. Our happy genes are designed to counterbalance our sad (depressive) genes. Happy genes need competition to survive but we should not allow this genetic competition to be used for purposes other than for survival. If there was no competition, they would lose their survival skills and atrophy. Too much competition is caused by stress, greed, and our inability to adjust to the modern overabundance of food in most of the world. Our genes are still trying to adapt to a time when the scarcity of food required us to eat too much in order to store up carbohydrates. This is Darwinism on an acceptable Christian platform because survival of the fittest does not mean that God did not create Man. The happy gene is located in the pleasure center of the brain and it is manipulating our senses to eat more than we should and this must be blamed on the gene because FW cannot alter the genetic code. In addition, our unconscious mind is playing tricks on us by fooling us into thinking that if we eat from a smaller plate, we are eating less food. This also can't be attributed to FW because we don't know what our subconscious mind is thinking. Watching TV makes us subconsciously eat more. Eating with large groups tends to make us eat more. Our hunter/gatherer ancestors were required to eat as much high calorie foods as they could find to survive. They needed lots of energy to run and fight. They did not have to worry about high levels of blood glucose because they were always on the move. Today our genes still crave high calorie foods not because of survival but because sugar and fat foods make our happy genes happy. And this craving is addictive. The more we eat the more we want. The higher the glucose level, to a point, the more pleasure, i.e., the more happiness. But the pay back of this pleasure is costly. As glucose level falls, the happy genes start complaining and want more

> "*A subconscious alert to death causes us to seek God and triggers a conscious alert that causes us to seek a burial policy.*"
> SAM SHIPLEY

pleasure/happiness and the cycle continues. All of the above pertain to behavior outside the control of FW. There may be a hidden gem here that we are overlooking. If we would quit "babying" our happy gene and be satisfied with less happiness, but just enough to keep the gene competitive, we could actually be happier than we are. As odd as this sounds, this is what genetic research is telling us. To use the sugar analogy as proof, we eat more to be happier but the result is becoming less happy. This would apply across the board to other things that make us happy. In the many documentaries I have seen of over-weight people, none of them seem to be happy. In going deeper, let's see what the Bible says: Matt. 6:19 states "Do not store up for yourselves treasures" (do I dare say 'happiness) "on earth, where moth and rust destroy and where thieves break in and steal." And Matt. 6:20 states "But store up for yourselves treasures in Heaven, where neither moth nor rust destroy, and where thieves do not break in or steal." A problem occurs when we look for happiness in the wrong place. Our brain is hardwired to seek happiness and when it can't find it, our physical and psychosomatic diseases such as depression, compulsive addition, pain, stress, and anxiety come into play. An entire book could be written on the implications of our brains being hardwired for its need for happiness. We were born into sin and until saved, were left to flounder in the quicksand of our sin nature. When we fell from His grace, we lost everything of value except for one thing, our ability to seek happiness. Sin left us with the inability to do anything good in God's eyes. I claim that happiness and FW are diametrically opposed. The happy gene is an innate gem given to us by God <u>while we were yet sinners and for which we did not have to wait for salvation to use.</u> I claim that God did this in order to ensure posterity of the human race. Lab experiments using rats have proven that when their brain functions have been altered, they cannot reproduce even though their reproductive organs were intact. Our genes are indirectly telling us to not be so happy, nutritional science is telling us that gluttonous living is one of the deadly sins, Hindus are telling us to not seek happiness from the world but to look inward, the Bible tells us that true happiness is stored up for us in Heaven, and Solomon tells us that riches and toil are vanity (Ecclesiastes 1:2), which is a disappointment to those who think that it takes at least some money to be happy. And lastly, my Mom and Dad told me how to be austere in order to be happy. I will leave this research with something I did not have before. I am going to cancel our family vacation and tell the kids it is best to be less happy by eating broccoli and green beans instead of pizza because they will get all the pizza they want in Heaven and will have a vacation every day. With the way science is running away with itself, I am serious when I say the next breakthrough will be how to modify the happy gene and live according to the new genetic code which will enable us to eat anything we want and not get fat without having to wait until Heaven.

One aspect of unknown causes is complicated and will not be adequately addressed in this book, i.e., what about a sin I committed long ago and knew it was a sin? God has forgiven me but I have forgotten what it was and it is in my unconscious mind. Both science and the Bible support my belief that the subconscious mind does not have a delete button. Our conscious mind does. Our subconscious mind bears witness to both good and bad things we did. It's hard to imagine that our fragile mind and brain is indelible. The Bible teaches that every act we do is recorded and we will be held accountable but we must align this teaching with those acts

> "But we are bound to give thanks always to God for you, brethren beloved of the Lord, because God hath from the beginning chosen you to salvation..."
>
> II THESS. 2:13

for which we are not held accountable which are those autonomic acts caused by our subconscious mind. In defining the above "accountable", it is pertaining to crowns in heaven or blessings on earth, not salvation. Our sins are forgiven but good and bad deeds are tallied to determine rewards. We will forget things in our lifetimes but at the Judgement, all things will be remembered. For Christians, this accountability refers to rewards gained or lost. Satan is always reminding me of my sins of long ago so those memories are still there. God forgave me but I may not have forgiven myself. Is it possible a long-ago event sublimely effects and influences my decisions today? Yes, if we will take note that science is telling us an event is always there and its purpose is to be bought into play when needed. If this influence resulted in a positive effect, it would be easy to say that both God and I forgave this sin. But if I didn't forgive myself, my past sin(s) remains as a haunting and self-destructive mechanism that Satan so conveniently bears witness to. Isaiah 1:18 tells us our sins are "as white as snow." This speaks to God's forgiveness but does not inform about the harm we do to ourselves. In summary, we are responsible for our conscious actions. For our unconscious behavior, a Christian will be told by the Holy Spirit that what he did was wrong. He doesn't have to know what unconsciously *caused* him to be afraid of the dark but will be responsible for its *effects*. (if he steels a flashlight) I am convinced that God sometimes shows us causes that we are not aware of, and obviously, these we are responsible for. We are made complex in His image but not made to understand this complexity. Science is busy making oil-based fertilizers and pesticides, massive dams and irrigation systems, medicines that have increased our life spans, and have at least doubled our food production. Science has done all these great things and now it's trying to bury our most cherished possession, our FW, our belief that the cause of our behavior originates within our consciousness. But science will not be able to convince the theological community to give up FW; it's doing its job by bridging the gap between the conscious and subconscious minds and its beginning to connect the subconscious mind to the spiritual dimension that heretofore (before gene mapping) had not been seen. The discoveries taking place in the inner recesses of our mind are a giant step forward taking place right here on earth. For those who believe in bondage of the will, (Calvinism) it creates a dilemma, but one that can be resolved, about how responsible we are for our behavior if we are not aware of what initially caused it. But much of our behavior has nothing to do with our moral or spiritual responsibility. We go to work, buy groceries, go to bed...

MIND/BRAIN AND UNIVERSE

Every act in the universe has multiple causes. The laws that govern our brain and the laws that govern our universe share the same multiple cause characteristic. Our intangible wills are governed by these same laws. Our brain and mind functions are a microcosm of the universe. Our brain is a small physical universe and reacts to a cause in a domino effect fashion similar to planetary bodies. Our mind is similar to the yet unknown characteristics of the universe's black hole. In the universe, a cause could start when a planet disintegrates and its small pieces coalesce until a new planet is formed. Gravity can cause a small dark hole to form and other causes can contribute to the enlargement of the hole. Or a lack of gravity can create dark energy or dark holes. In our brain a similar occurrence takes place when certain parts of our brain can be damaged and to some extent, can be repaired. Some neurons can be restored. In the universe, gravity can cause a small dark hole to form which is followed by other causes that contribute to the enlargement of the hole. In our brain, irreparable holes can form. These changes in the universe are mirrors of our mind in two ways, (1) as we compare our conscious mind, in which we are able to see and examine its functions, with the visible universe in which we are able to see and examine its functions and (2), as we compare our unconscious mind, in which we know so little, to the dark holes in space, in which we know even less. This analogy is my supposition and is not supported by science but the parallels bear striking resemblances.

The mother of invention is necessity. At some point in the mind of Man, he had to be asking, "Why is the earth flat?" "If there is a God, why doesn't He show Himself?" And the really big question before religion became organized, "Is there an afterlife?" As religion began to take shape, a paramount question arose and still continues today. (FW) "Why do some people go to Hell and some to Heaven?" Before the Old Testament was written, the Hebrew culture passed its belief on orally. Some cultures that never became Christian asked these same transcendental questions because we know that most cultures searched for an afterlife explanation. A brief introduction to ancient man and religion shows us that 100,000 years ago Neanderthals were burying their dead along with various items of jewelry and other personal items. Since they knew the body did not go anywhere, this indicates they believed in an afterlife. About 11,000 years ago, a structure known as the " Gobekli TepeTemplein Turkey",

> "*Without some form of adversity, we would have no motivation.*"
> SAM SHIPLEY

(spelling doublechecked) was built that looked like a religious structure. Since cities did not begin to appear until thousands of years later, this is probably evidence that a spiritual culture preceded civilization.

Historians believe that monotheistic religions first appeared 5,000 years ago. I am suggesting that this may have been the time when the idea of FW emerged and am guessing that religions having multi-gods did not have a FW theology. As Man's brain began to adjust itself to his environment, he easily saw the principle of cause and effect operating around him. To him cause and effect and FW were probably the same thing. This is the best that I or anyone else can do in an attempt to know the beginning of FW before the written word was established. When he threw a rock, the bird fell. He applied what he knew to answer questions he did not know. In his existential world, cause and effect were easily recognized in everything he knew and did. After Man learned to survive, there was an insatiable and unrelenting need to know why an apple falls and why do some go to Heaven and some to Hell or at least what happens after death. We know this because archeology shows how our brains evolved and we know that the above questions are pertinent to our developing brain. It is scientifically correct to say that Adam's brain was biologically different than that of modern man. This is proven by research that shows how environment shapes our brain. It is also correct to say that modern man's brain is constantly undergoing physical changes in size and neural replacement and displacement. Images comparing a veteran's brain, suffering from PTSD, is remarkedly different than the brain of someone who does not have PTSD. Considering the changing size of the brain is important in order to understand that as the brain size changes, so does behavior. The

> *"Without some degree of uncertainty, man would have never left his cave."*
> SAM SHIPLEY

human brain has undergone evolutionary changes resulting from environmental influences and these changes have resulted in changes in behavior. FWers credit these changes to FW.

At some point when ancient man was gazing at the stars, he combined what he knew about cause and effect with what he knew about his determination and will power and how his determination in doing something resulted in positive behavior. He would have had to see the relationship between a cause and its effect and would have assumed, erroneously, that he was the primary cause that caused the effect, and therefore would have believed that he was the master of his destiny and in control of his will, at least to the permissive extent of the gods or God he worshipped. Modern research proves that Man's higher brain capacity enables him to believe in the existence of a being higher than himself. Cause and effect and FW counterman each other but it is easy to mistake them as partners. This is how FW, as we know it today, was invented. I use the above imaginary scenario because it's been difficult to find FW in secular recorded history except for books pertaining to mythology. Regardless of when it came into use, it fulfilled a much needed purpose in Man's early existence and its usefulness continued past the Enlightenment Period and on into the nineteen eighties when gene mapping and brain imagining began to tell us what our conscious and subconscious minds were saying. It was at this point that science encroached on the validity of FW and its usefulness should have ended. In earlier days, Augustine, Calvin, and Luther did their part to destroy FW, but following this, science failed to gain the upper hand. Science replaced the flat world theory which stood for centuries but could make no headway against FW. Before FW was proved invalid it served a useful purpose by acting as a relief valve for the purpose of relieving stress. But the truth about science and bondage (anti-FW) and cause and effect don't have to stand in the way of relieving stress. Stress relief can be achieved through other outlets. For the Christian, prayer is just one of the answers. Research in psychology has shown that when a person cannot find a reasonable and ready answer or solution to a pressing problem, he employs the mother of invention and invents a stress reducing solution. In many cases, this results in solutions heavy in quackery but it works. Unrelieved stress results in shorter live spans. People don't want to know a truth if it infringes on a long-held belief. At funerals, preachers relieve the stress of loved ones by encouraging the belief that the deceased is waiting in Heaven. But since everyone is not going to Heaven, this is another myth attached to FW. And practically all kids are told that death results in Heaven. Therefore FW does serve a purpose if you believe that not knowing the truth is worth a somewhat longer lifespan. The other side of the coin is a person can somehow offset stress regardless of the truth and still have a longer life span. The idea of FW came before the Bible was written as evidenced by many non- Christian cultures that taught it. In the Christian West, we were introduced to FW in the Bible when we read about Lucifer's Fall. Isaiah 14:12 tells us "How you have fallen from Heaven, O star of the morning, son of the dawn. You have been cut down to the earth. You who have weakened the nations!" And 14-13 says "But you said in your heart, I will ascend to Heaven. I will raise my throne above the stars of God." 14-14 states "I will make myself like the Most High." For Lucifer to say these grandiose things and think that he could usurp God leads me to believe that he had FW and supports the idea that God originated and established FW in Heaven that paralleled FW in the pre-Fall Garden. When he was cast down to earth, minus his FW, Satan became a slave to the sin he created, thus beginning his earthly career as both a slave to, and a master of, sin. FW cannot be adequately understood without tracing its beginning in Heaven with Lucifer and it's ending on earth with Adam. Sin deprived Lucifer of his FW in Heaven and on earth and deprived Adam of his FW on earth, therefore creating a cause and effect link between sin and FW. To couch this in its historical context, where FW went, it opened the door to sin. This is proven by God giving pre-Fall Adam FW and Adam freely choosing sin. (disobedience) But a new day has dawned with the death and resurrection of Jesus. Christians are now free indeed but it's a new type of freedom never before seen. Pre-Fall Adam did not have it because when he sinned, he lost his eternal life. Christians are blessed with a new type of freedom that Lucifer and Adam did not have. For Christians, eternal death is not possible. 1 Cor. 15:55-56 tells us "O death, where is your victory? O death, where is your sting? The sting of death is sin, and the power of sin is the law." Probably more than any other scripture, the above verses establish a kinship between FW and sin. From FWs beginning in Heaven, it had two faces, one good when it was used for good as God intended, and one bad, when used for sin as Satan intended. God knew that when he gave FW, man would mess it up. FW could be described as sin's older brother because FW came before sin. God did not create sin but He did create its penalty and now that the Law has been nullified, the old FW has been modified and the new FW is free of unforgivable sin, its former brother. All the above pertain to salvation and cast the Christian as someone who sins but is not a sinner.

Dr. Andrew Newburg, in his course guide to the *Spiritual Brain: Science and Religious Experience,* tells us that the psychology and scientific definition of myth, "does not imply falsehood". He explained that in many contexts throughout history, myth is a powerful story that explains the world to us. We create myths in order to explain to ourselves what cannot be explained with logic and reason. In this sense, Moses' trip to the top of Mt. Sinai would be a myth even if the story was true and would still be a myth if it wasn't. Fact or fiction is irrelevant. This may not agree with the dictionary definition but Newberg's understanding of myth is that it is necessary in order for us to gain a meaning or insight into important events. He believes the limitations of our brain make it necessary for us to create myths. He believes that what we perceive is a second-hand rendition of what is actually happening. This reinforces

> *"The only place certainty will exist is Heaven but in eternity, certainty has no Meaning."*
> SAM SHIPLEY

other claims in this book proving that we are only capable of consciously absorbing and receiving five percent of what is seen, heard, and thought. We can extrapolate his findings to say that of the vast universe of both space and mind, we must attempt to garner some meaning of this vastness with a limited amount of information. With this in mind, I can easily see why our brains are designed to create myths. Short of apologizing for FW, I can justify to some extend the need for it early on in man's history but in regards to modern man and science, justification is not possible. In the sixteenth century, Erasmus, a monk, and Martin Luther's emesis, championed FW. At that time, lacking science, it is understandable that he was able to make FW believable.

Man's will should be defined in three ways. The first is an unsaved man's will is in bondage to Satan. Ephesians 2:2 tells us "…in which you formally walked according to the course of this world, according to the prince of the power of the air, of the spirit that is now working in the sons of disobedience." The Calvinistic view of this scripture teaches that an unsaved person's will does not have the capability of making any godly choices or actions until God intervenes and buys back from Satan some of the sons of disobedience. This buy back is necessary because we were all, at one time, properties of Satan. God appointed Satan to his princely kingdom and ownership of its earthly unsaved inhabitants. In Genesis, we are told that when Adam ate from the Tree, he would die. This surely means that Adam's dead soul and all mankind sold itself into slavery to Satan. This happened when Adam voluntarily chose to die; spiritually dead people are his property. The only way this death can be reversed and bought back is by the blood and death and resurrection of Jesus.

The second definition of man's will is borrowed from Luther's book, "Bondage of the Will" and the scripture it contains. He quotes Paul's role as being the bond servant of Christ. One of the characteristics of being a bond servant and bought by Christ's blood is that the status of Paul's will, and ours, has reverted to the FW status of pre-Fall Adam, except for one difference. Pre-Fall Adam had the FW ability to disobey

> *"Do not waste the crisis in your life. Make it count for something."*
>
> SAM SHIPLEY

God and lose his eternal life. That's no longer possible, according to Luther and Calvin's interpretation of the Bible, but according to FW theology, the FW of pre-Fall and post-Fall Adam and Adam's prodigy has changed little. In contrast, the Bible teaches that the descendants of Adam who became Christians are a new breed. A new type of FW should be recognized, one I will label as The Free Will of Christ in Us and one that Reformed Churches would probably agree with. John 8:36 tells us "So if the Son makes you free, you will be free indeed." 8:35-37 states "The slave does not remain in the house forever; the son does remain forever. So, if the Son makes you free, you will be free indeed." It must be noted that this is not the kind of FW I adamantly oppose. The erroneous kind of FW claims that our freedom comes from within us but the Bible teaches the real freedom comes from Christ in us. Job 8:9 tells us who we are and how we came to be that way. "For we are only of yesterday and know nothing because our days on earth are as a shadow." This verse tells us our short duration on earth is not the only reason we know nothing. The strong implication is we know nothing because we don't have the inner knowledge in and of ourselves through FW. Paul probably had the word "shadow" in mind in reference to his "see through the glass darkly." There is not even a hint of FW activity here. Job 8:10 tells us where our knowledge comes from and it's not from within ourselves, not from FW, to wit "Will they not teach you and tell you and bring forth words from their minds." This is undoubtedly referring to learning from a source coming from outside. Verse 8:11 says "Can the papyrus grow up without marsh? Can the rushes grow without water?" These verses clearly establish cause and effect as the impetus and prime mover and is opposed to everything that FW stands for.

The third definition of man's will is characterized by normal, everyday behavior and is the subject of scientific scrutiny centered around the relationship between the conscious and subconscious minds. This scientific inquiry is trying to avoid any relationship between religious FW and secular behavior but

> "*Wisdom is greater than knowledge because wisdom includes knowledge and the due use of it.*"
> JOSEPH BURRITT SEVEL CAPPONI

the similarities are becoming more apparent. In the early nineteen hundreds, Sigmund Freud taught the unconscious mind was analogous to an iceberg. The most important part of the iceberg, the part that plays the major role, is the part that can't be seen. It has the larger mass and therefore accounts for the majority of its behavior. The most important part of our brain, (the unconscious mind) the part that plays the major role, is the part that couldn't be seen in Freud's day. Freud believed the unconscious part of our mind plays the major role. Today's brain imaging shows scientists what goes on (at least in part) in the mind/ brain complex when activity is being processed. The conscious part of our mind plays the lesser role. In Freud's time, the lack of imagining technology delayed more compelling research. The unconscious mind is the regulatory part that controls our conscious mind. Freud was ahead of his time in this regard by positing that the unconscious mind told the conscious mind what to do. Today's neuroscientists agree. Today we can correlate his analogy to cause and effect. Traumatic events stored in the subconscious is the cause and the changes in the brain circuitry is the effect. Now with brain circuitry technology, we can prove it. Gene mapping of the brain has shown that we have separate conscious and unconscious image feedback although it is possible they both reside in the same region. Medical technology will hopefully develop better treatment for illnesses such as depression and PTSD because we know that extreme traumatic experiences are stored in the unconscious mind and lay dormant until leaked, for lack of a better word, into the conscious mind which results in a psychosomatic episode. To complete the picture of the mind/brain configuration, the books I have read list an additional part of the mind called the preconscious mind that serves as a way station between the conscious and unconscious.

In a movie, Jack Nickelson said "You can't handle the truth." The reason God created us with an unconscious mind, which keeps us mostly in the dark, is if we consciously knew and recognized the actual causes and truth behind all our lifetime behavior, we couldn't handle it. Conscious thoughts are in bondage to its slave-master, the unconscious mind. It is impossible for a conscious thought to be original. When I consciously see a red barn, that is not the first time I saw a red barn. In order to recognize it as a red barn, I would have had to have seen a red barn previously. If I had never seen a red barn, my unconscious mind would have had to piece together something red I had seen in the past with a structure I had previously identified as something that looked like a barn. The result would not have been an original image. Its composite whole would have consisted of sub-parts which they themselves would have been borrowed and stored. If I had never seen the color red or a structure, (which would have been impossible to draw a blank on both color and structure) my subconscious mind would borrow memories of similar things. Every conscious thought we have is based on or caused by something historical, something that has happened in the past. That is to say, even though I am thinking in the present tense, I could not have formulated that thought from nothing. I have to have a past existence in order to create a present existence. When I say "I love you," this is not original because agape love originated from God. I am simply borrowing something and passing it on to you. No matter what I say, it could not be original because every word I speak or think comes from an established language format, which in turn had to come from something previous to that.

> "*Adam's creation was God's best. His fall was Adam's worst.*"
>
> SAM SHIPLEY

I don't believe we can think an original thought because of the trillions of people who have come before us. Even with the advent of new words, technology, and ideas, it's hard to think of something original. The only way to have an original thought is to have a lobotomy and wipe everything in the brain out but starting with a blank mind would result in a blank thought. This is more than conjecture on my part. It has been done on animals. Most of the stuff in our past is junk. I should not dwell on why I did not get that promotion years ago and when I dream about it, I wake up mad. God wants us to concentrate on what's in front and not our subconscious which faces backward. Science has not yet gotten to the bottom of what happens when the subconscious interacts with the conscious. When we spend too much time consciously looking back, it interferes with future plans. Some retrospect is needed but living too much in the past in order to correct mistakes that God is not concerned about is a waste of time.

Regrettably, I do that too much and that is just on some of those things that my subconscious sometimes bring to the surface. For those who have the time to ponder such things, we are constantly living in the immediate past because by the time the future gets here, it is history. This can't be avoided but spending too much time in the distant past can be. I can't claim originality for any of the above but neither can I cite their source because these claims are based on years of reading which was stored in my subconscious and now is coming to light when I need it. If you agree with me, I have accomplished my goal in giving a new insight (but not original) into the meaning of originality, borrowing, and plagiarism.

Einstein's general theory of relativity has a mathematical formula that explains the spacetime phenomena and how spacetime is curved and bent and how the past and present seem to reverse themselves. We are not born with a blank mind so even infants have a past and present. At birth, the infant is full of prenatal influences. FWers are faced with absolute proof that FW is a bogus belief but they are never phased in their resolute belief. What more or better proof is needed to kill this belief than a prenatal's exposure to its mother's secluded environment. There is no FW here and as the baby is born and grows, it does not pick up FW down the road, either. The FWers attempt to argue that FW grows as the baby grows does not stand up to scrutiny because a sixty-year old's FW would have to be stronger than that of a thirty- year old. A baby's brain is a sponge ready to absorb as much as possible, but its conscious mind is a porous sponge at best. Elsewhere in this book, mention is made of research that proves that our conscious mind only absorbs five percent of everything going on around us. The rest of our environmental bombardment is dumped into an indelible subconscious storage tank. Reflecting on the past does have its uses but one of them should not being occupied with thoughts of what could have been. The Bible tells us we are new creatures. "New" signifies a conscious future. A Christian's sinful past should be permeated with thoughts of being a new creature. That is to say, more time should be spend on being a new creature and less or none on reliving things that could have been. This is not an easy thing to do. This is why Paul tells us to take on the breastplate of righteousness. The meaning I get is a breastplate worn in physical battle is heavy in order to provide the protection we need to turn the sharp arrows. When we take our mind off Jesus, we don't have protection from Satan's arrows and we become heavy. "Therefore, if anyone is in Christ, he is a new creature; the old things passed away; behold, new things have come," Corinthians 5:17. We are constantly fighting a battlefield of the mind. We cannot interpret "old things passed away" as meaning that our indelible subconscious mind passes away. Paul said to leave behind those things of the past but this does not mean that Satan voluntarily will leave them behind. Jesus told Satan to get behind Him and this is not just referring to a physical proximity. It informs me that Jesus put Satan out of His conscious mind and serves as a model for us to do the same. The reason God created us with a conscious mind is to enable us to put one foot after the other and go forward. God will help us recall selective events of the past that will not overwhelm us and use for His glory. Jesus said to let today's worries go and deal with them later. The Bible calls worry a sin, when it harms the body, in both the Old and New Testaments, because our bodies are the Temple of God, not to be harmed. Paul tells us to forget our troublesome past. When I begin to lose sight of God, Satan always reminds me of my mistakes. We were designed to stay in motion and that's what our conscious mind is for. Our subconscious mind is for both sleeping and directing our conscious behavior. Sleep walking is an example of an overzealous subconscious mind that takes over the role of the conscious mind. Even in sleep, we are working. If we knew the "why" or cause of everything we had done, we would become little gods in knowledge but imbecilic in the application of knowledge. Since the subconscious is the workhorse, it has to be included in the definition of knowledge. So how could we *handle* all the unconscious knowledge? The Bible tells us we are new creatures and science tells us that our subconscious mind represents the old creature and the Bible joins this chorus in Matthew 12:36 by telling us "But I tell you that every careless word that people speak, they shall give an accounting for it in the day of judgement." There is no way I can consciously remember every careless word I have said but they are stored in my subconscious mind and the above scripture is one more proof of the biblical existence of the subconscious mind. "New" signifies a conscious future. The past is signified by our subconscious past. The Bible tells us we see through a glass darkly and the context of this refers to the weakness of our conscious mind because we don't consciously see through our subconscious mind. When I begin to lose sight of God, Satan always reminds me of my mistakes. We were designed to stay in motion and the conscious mind was designed for this purpose. If we are not eating or sleeping, we are thinking about something. Even in sleep, we are working. The Bible warns us about the increase of knowledge in later days and this is referring to just conscious knowledge. So how could we *handle* all the unconscious knowledge? If we knew all the causes and truth that drove us, we would be completely immobilized and unable to concentrate. Our brains are huge storage bins but not that huge. In Genesis 3:22, God prevented fallen Adam from eating of the Tree of Life and living forever. He had eaten from the Tree of Knowledge and it's a fact that he could not handle this knowledge because he immediately sinned. Does this relate to the Bible's warning of an increase in knowledge? With all the pass words I have to remember, I'm going crazy with just pass words, web sites, and stolen identities. Does Nickelson's famous line apply here?

God's plan of salvation and its relation to FW is addressed early on in Genesis 3:22. His plan is there is only one way to be saved, through the Door of Jesus. (John 10:9) "I am the door; anyone who enters through Me will be saved". I extrapolate this to mean that we enter through the will of Jesus, not through FW because other scripture makes it clear that God gives the saved to Him. The reason God prevented Adam from eating from the Tree (Jesus) and

> "One way to get to the top is push someone else up." *Newspaper*

regaining eternal life is He had previously pronounced Adam's spiritual death. Allowing him to eat from the Tree would have countermanded this death. We don't know if Adam became saved but if he did, he and the trillion or so who died before Jesus' resurrection were saved on credit, so to speak, and were allowed to posthumously walk through the Door. Therefore, it was not time for Adam to know Jesus. This informs that fallen Man can't handle the Tree of Knowledge of Good and Evil and the Tree of Life, without God's help, after having lost the gift of FW. God was not ready to offer His Son for salvation based on grace at that time. The Law of Moses was not yet available. Salvation was based on the coming Law of Moses and after the Cross, was based on grace. What would be the purpose of The Cross if God had permitted Adam, and corporately Man, to eat of the Tree of Life and live forever before Jesus had the opportunity to die or before the initiation of the Law. Our salvation by grace can only come through His death and resurrection. FW can't be added to this formula because there is nothing free about salvation. Jesus paid for it on the Cross. If Adam had been permitted to eat the Tree of Life at that time in his fallen state, he would have regained his eternal life, obviated Jesus's' death, and countermanded God's decree of death. The only way we are permitted to live forever is to accept Christ's substitutionary death, which obviously at the time, Jesus had not died. Adam had FW before the Fall. If he had been permitted to eat of the Tree of Life after the Fall, he would have regained his eternal life and FW. In regards to the pre-Fall Garden, eternal life and FW were synonymous. We inherited Adam's sin when he fell. If he had not fallen, it's conjecture to say we would have inherited eternal life but the subjective inference is there. The fact that he lost his eternal life and this loss was passed on makes it hypothetically possible to believe the opposite, that if he had maintained his eternal life, it would have been passed on. I acknowledge this is a mouthful but some FWers believe in universal salvation where everybody will be saved. The only way one can live forever is to be redeemed. God did not design a universal door. Everyone interprets many parts of the Bible differently, depending on their worldview. To be clear, I am not saying that our uniqueness gives us the right to claim our status as an original "causer". I make this claim to establish what *might* be my unique worldview or perspective. I say "might" because I have not read every book or narrative and it could be possible that someone else has this same worldview. I claim that each one of us has a little piece of some aspect of our worldview that is unique but not original. My unique worldview is as follows: <u>FW and eternal life were inseparable elements in the pre-Fall Garden and when one of them fell, so did the other.</u> I want to establish this claim chronologically, similar to when a door is closed, it is followed by the click of the latch, i.e., when the door of life was closed to Adam, it was closely followed by the closing of FW, or both occurred at the same time. It is not happenstance that before the Fall, FW and eternal life coexisted.

Proof of FW's existence. During Adam's tenure in the Garden, the only thing he was required to do, which was a restriction of his will, was not eat from the Tree of Knowledge of Good and Evil, Gen. 2:17. In Gen. 1:28, God listed their duties such as be fruitful and multiply, rule, and subdue, but these functions cannot be construed as requirements or limitations placed on their will, but rather as a blessing that enhanced their FW.

Proof of Adam's possible eternal life. Gen. 2:17 tell us that Adam would surely die if he ate of the Tree … This is an unmistakable promise of eternal life if he did not eat and just as unmistakable is the promise that his eternal life was contingent on his FW ability to keep it.

When Adam lost his FW. When he ate from the Tree of Knowledge of Good and Evil, as evidenced by 3:17, to paraphrase: The ground was cursed and full of thorns and thistles and he was given a life sentence of hard labor (toil) without possibility of parole. This has to be describing bondage to sin *yet the FWer in the furthest reach of the wildest imagination insists this miserable existence embodies that of FW.* 3:17 and other scriptures show what FW and eternal life was before and after the Fall. Before the Fall, all Adam had to do was not eat from the tree. This was the only limitation to his FW. The first three chapters of Genesis shows what it's like to live in paradise. He could wrestle with his bears and run with his

> "When you tell me you don't know or care, this tells me you are both ignorant and apathetic and I don't care if you don't care, which makes me intelligently apathetic." Sam Shipley

cheetahs. Every modern man would love this. Eve also had a blissful environment with the promise of pain free childbearing. Genesis tells us this in detail. After the Fall, he was sentenced to hard labor for life (he lived to be nine hundred and thirty) with no holidays or week-ends off, followed by death with no possibility of parole except maybe God's grace. Modern criminals have it much easier. They may get death but no hard labor. Even the most determined man would agree this was a long time to quarrel with a wife and hack out a living or a long time for a wife to put up with her husband. In addition, he had to fight for his life to keep the animals from killing him (they no longer belonged to him and his dominion over them weakened), raise his unruly kids, hide from God, endure the murder of his son Abel, and according to Gen. 4:14, watch as Cain tried to escape death from his neighbors. I live in a relatively good neighborhood yet Adam's life and misfortunes are a cariture of what is seen every day throughout my neighborhood. In a poorer neighborhood, the misfortunes of modern living are seen more frequently. *Yet the FWer continues to insist that poverty and hunger are obstacles to overcome through the auspices of FW and refuse to recognize the difference between bondage to sin and the freedom gained from being a bond servant to Christ.* Adam's post Fall life parallels that of modern man. I claim that Adam's and our predicament started when Adam lost his FW and eternal life. When you factor in sin, the loss of Adam's perfect Garden, and the traumatic events of all of today's families, you will agree that my depiction of Adam's loss of eternal life and being kicked out of Eden is not exaggerated and lines up with scripture and with today's modern world filled with trouble. My next-door neighbor, who is a school consular, told me that she does not know a single child in school that does not have family problems and she does not have a single relative, including in-laws, who do not have problems with addiction, marriage, illness, depression, etc.

When Adam lost his eternal life. When he ate from the Tree of Knowledge of Good and Evil, as evidenced by 3:16 and 3:17.

When he lost both eternal life and FW. This was a simultaneous event as proven by the above scriptures and was not a coincidence that both just happened to expire at the same time and proves my claim that one is contingent on the existence of the other. Another scriptural confirmation of the inseparability of FW and eternal life is 3:22, "Then the Lord God said, 'Behold, the man has become like one of Us, knowing good and evil, and now, lest he stretch out his hand, and take also from the tree of life, and eat, and live forever." This clearly states that God denied him eternal life, to paraphrase "lest he eat and live forever." Just as clear is God's termination of Adam's FW," "...lest he stretch out his hand....." The "lest he" emphatically defines what pre-Fall FW was, i.e., he could have stretched out his hand (this signifies FW) and eaten from the Tree of Life. This explains God's opposition to FW by eliminating the possibility of Adam using FW to reestablish his eternal life. This is exactly what FWers claim they can do today: Chose God without any help from God. God is not going to reestablish the type of FW that Adam had before the Fall. The sad thing about this claim is the only difference between then and now is the Cross, and it's the Cross, not FW, that enables Man to "stretch out his hand" to eat of the Tree of Life (The Cross). The point must be made that our ability to stretch out our hand comes from God, not FW. God prevented Adam from stretching out his hand and eating from the Tree of Life after he lost his FW (Genesis 3:22) but FWers ignore this truth and continue to argue FWs existence. The above represents a fresh insight that I don't believe can be found in other books. This exegesis applied to FW and eternal life tells us the condition in which FW, modified to meet the post Fall environment and eternal life, can exist today by Christians becoming bond servants to Christ, who will set us free. None of the Reformed churches or Calvinistic narratives I have read interpret Genesis by linking the pre-Fall FW with post-Fall bondage of the will but in my opinion, the link is clear. Bondage represents a different kind of freedom than the pre-Fall free will that Adam had. Many Christians, including FWers, do not believe that being a bond servant to Christ makes us free and believe that it's their FW that enables them to be a bond servant. This teaching omits Christ as the enabler and replaces Him with FW. The Bible teaches that Christ's bond servants have been sealed. Revelations 7:3 tells us "...until we have sealed the bond-servants of our God...." Many scriptures define seal as irrevocable as opposed to the teachings of FW, which defines salvation as a come and go gift which can be received or returned depending on the dictates of FW and in effect, describes the gift of salvation as not sealed and is like trying on a pair of shoes that don't fit and taking them back. Paul tells us this is the only way to be truly free. John 8:36 tells us "So if the Son makes you free, you will be free indeed." The gift of freedom for a Christian when he becomes saved is not the same FW that existed in the Garden. God is not going to allow another Fall. We fell once and would fall again if given the chance. The Garden Pre-Fall FW permitted Adam to choose to lose eternal life as evidenced by God allowing him to eat of the Tree. The fascinating message here is he was permitted to eat of the Tree of Life and refused before he ate of the Tree of Knowledge of Good and Evil. This pre-Fall Garden shows how powerful FW was in its heyday. I believe it was a way for God to impress us how dangerous it is to be without His intervention and support. Adam's FW did not serve his or our best interest. I treat pre-Fall FW like Paul treats the Law. They both served a purpose. This does not mean that God's FW design was imperfect. Note that before sin entered, Adam was like a small child that requires parental care and guidance. When a child requires guidance, he is not thrown out of the house but if he rejects guidance, he must leave. The freedom chosen Christians have does not allow them the option to deny or reject eternal life. If this option was available, we could start the pre-Fall Garden all over again, which would start the post-Fall Garden all over again. 2 Corinthians 1:22

> *"Endorphins lessen pain by stimulating you to feel better. I construe this to be like taking a pain killer and slapping yourself hard enough to override the pain?"*
> SAM SHIPLEY

states, "who also sealed us and gave us the Spirit in our hearts as a pledge." Adam was made perfect, but God did not seal his eternal life. Today's salvation seal prevents a replay and seals in concrete the difference between pre-Fall FW and post-Fall bondage freedom in Christ. God's purpose in allowing the Fall is to give us a preview of Heaven by way of the pre-Fall Garden and a full feature showing what this intolerable world is without Him in the post-Fall world. Before the Fall, Adam had a one hundred percent tax free entitlement to eternal life. After the Fall, we are taxed to the hilt and lost our entitlement because it cost Jesus His blood.

A study published in the journal *Addiction,* May, 2005, shows the subtle but absolute influence caused by the power of subliminal suggestion and is just one more study proving the fallibility of FW. This study proves the effectiveness of suggestions used by marketing in the TV advertising industry in which millions of dollars are spent verifying the efficacy of behavior caused by subconscious decisions that have nothing to do with the conscious decision making associated with the alleged efficacy of FW. The men in this study were college students and were asked if they thought that alcohol contributes to a sexual drive and most thought it did. They were then subliminally exposed to words associated with alcohol such as "booze", "drunk", etc. They were then shown photos of woman and were asked to rate their attractiveness on a point scale. Most who thought that alcohol was a contributing factor rated the women as attractive. Those who did not think that alcohol was a contributing factor rated the women as less attractive. It was not FW that caused the men to think that the women were attractive. It was the clever joining of a conscious opinion with an unconscious suggestion that caused the men to think the women were attractive. This study proves the men did not freely think they were attractive but were caused to believe this from a source outside their control. This proves that alcohol consumption is not necessarily a causative agent in the sex drive pathway. On the humorist side, if a woman wants to attract a man, the study suggests it would help to have a "This Bud's for You" sign posted in her apartment. This may not help to get a husband, but it suggests that women may appear to be more attractive if they are dating men who think alcohol contributes to a sex drive. Sorry ladies but this study obviates FW as a viable factor and shows that our dating practices do not result in FW choices.

FWers and Calvinists agree that our worldview plays a role in our behavior because there is no denying that we are consciously aware of some of the things going on around us. The disagreement starts when a Calvinist states that our conscious will plays a secondary and subservient role to our unconscious will. FWers do not believe scientific proof that our unconscious will

> *"A government big enough to carry you is big enough to drop you."*
> SAM SHIPLEY

has the deciding vote in making choices and determining the primary cause of our behavior. I make a person mad and he claims I am insulting and condescending when I tell him he chose a Ford instead of a Dodge, *primarily* not because he liked its look and freely chose it (I agree he did like its look), but *primarily* because of an unconscious influence lurking in the background of his mind. In polite conversation, he will tolerate me with the unspoken question of how I can make such an assumption and not even know him. My answer is, "So it looks nice to you. How did you decide why it looks nice? Did it look nicer because the other models didn't look as nice?" I try to explain that a standard of what makes something look nice is a subjective criterion that did not originate in his conscious, or if you will, his FW mind. This criterion did not just pop into his mind automatically one day or appear from within his psyche without help from a source outside his conscious mind. It did not create itself and he did not create it. Wherever it came from, it took up residence in his subconscious mind. His thinking that it looked nice did not create itself nor was it created by his FW. I acknowledge that most people, outside academia, don't care about the difference between conscious and unconscious minds or the difference between primary and secondary causes. In discussing behavior with most people, little interest is shown in causes and brain functions and FW. Discussions concerning behavior is limited to easily discernable causes. I have an in-law who has a master's degree in clinical psychology and whose job is to treat abnormal behavioral problems like addiction or child abuse and she expresses little interest in subconscious behavior and does not seem to be aware of new research in regards to brain/mind discoveries, or at least does not show interest in what I consider to be earth shaking new research in neurology, sociology, or psychology. In doing her job, she does not need to know the subconscious mind determines behavior.

Science books tell us the only way to understand an atom is to dissect it. Dissection is also the only way to understand behavior. I have used several items like chairs and phones to dissect and understand behavior. None of the several items I have used to dispel FW came from books or articles. They must have come from logic or common sense originating from my unconscious mind. They did not come from or because of my FW. Just because I possess common sense and logic does not mean I caused them. My common sense was caused by my environment and my logic was caused by my education. Before leaving this topic, clarification must be given to the above statement that everything must have a cause. Astronomy is attempting to explain what caused the smallest particle and a step further, what caused dark energy and how did dark matter evolve. Non-Christian scientists are having a field day in hopes that something will be discovered that can't be explained as caused by God. The Big Bang Theory as caused by God is said to be in need of a physics overhaul and parallel universes are viewed as the next big discovery. For non-Christians, intelligent design needs a re-make and a way of making sense of chaos without relying on the existence of a higher being. But right here under our noses here on this planet is the biggest discovery, one bigger than the physical universe and one that entails the endless recesses of the mind. Is this a way for atheistic science to attempt to displace God as the Creator and Causer? Is there a way to explain how something can be caused by something that we did not know existed? In studying the science of the mind, our will could be better understood and social science could have a hand in world peace, feeding growing populations, and cultivating the kind of peace and happiness that God says we can have. This all despite the fact that we are heading for the last tribulation, where we will need His peace more than we ever have and can have peace regardless of the coming trials. This would be a discovery greater than anything we would find in outer space and parallel universes. In attempting to understand behavior, is there a form of behavior that is caused by something other than genes or environment or God that explains how a child raised in a loving family will pay this love forward? Or is there a way to explain how a lifelong Muslim chose God through the auspices of FW?

FW is free and valid in one sense of the word when examining the word "free". It is pseudo valid because millions of people think it is valid, and free because millions think it is free. FW has been monopolized by its users to mean that it has nothing to do with science or the interworking of the subconscious mind. I can say this with certainty because if it was possible to show a FWer the connection between the unconscious mind and the will, FW would have to be viewed in a different light. I am always looking for additional ways to disprove FW and it appears to me that the following constitutes another nail in the coffin of FW. Most people who believe in FW also believe there is an unconscious mind but do not see a viable and meaningful connection between the conscious mind and its enslavement to the unconscious. One way to connect the dots is to show the documented evidence of hypnosis. A person under hypnosis is said to be in a subconscious state and this would establish one of the dots. When the person under hypnosis complies with an instruction to lift his arm or repeat a word, this connects the other dot, thus proving that the unconscious mind overrides the conscious will. If overridden is too strong a word, it can be said that at least his unconscious mind was influenced to the point that a decision was made unconsciously outside the parameter of the conscious mind. However, I suspect that a FWer will reject this on the basis that compliance in a hypnotic state is in an artificial environment and therefore it doesn't work that way in the real world. But this is an exact model of the real world and this is how the real world works. Hypnosis shows the subconscious mind at work without the aid of MRIs. Freud and Luther would say that when we are in an unconscious state, we are in the real world. My sixty-year-old psychology book told me that our subconscious world is like a kitchen and is the busiest part of the house where so much of the living takes place and where all of the cooking is done. The word "cooking" is a perfect word for the processing of all the many daily events and the aroma really takes off as our subconscious mind is permeated with the many sounds and smells given to it by our daily existence. As stated earlier, God created us with two minds, one to maneuver us through the daily existential world and the unconscious mind to periodically exam and analysis the information stream in order to smooth out the wrinkles of life's problems and lessen its stresses. Science has proven that the unconscious mind can solve problems and conflicts that the conscious mind can't. All of us have proven that many times when we wake up and find a problem solved after a night of rest. Psychology teaches that unresolved crisis leads to a mental crisis. We have all experienced the conscious struggle in coping with a problem and the next morning, our subconscious "kitchen" had cooked up a solution.

For a period of time I dropped my routine reading of magazines about FW and the subconscious mind. Before I quit reading them, one article in the U.S. News and World Report, entitled *Mysteries of The Mind*, was the most informative piece of journalism I had read to date. Written in February 28, 2005, it addressed everything a non-scientist needed to know about what goes on in our brain concerning its FW and subconscious activity. Its six-page presentation was as comprehensive as six pages allow. If nothing else were ever written on the subject, this article heralded the fallacies of FW so effectively that the door is shut to any further contentious arguments regarding the legitimacy of FW yet in the twelve years since the article was written, there must undoubtedly be better articles written due to additional information on gene mapping and technical advances in brain imagining which have been added to an already conclusive array of brain research. The author of the article, Marianne Szegedy-Maszak, quotes neuroscientist Paul Whelan. "Much of what we do every minute of every day is unconscious. Life would be chaos if everything were on the forefront of our consciousness." I had come to this conclusion from reading previous articles regarding information that was stored in our subconscious mind and its role as the workhorse and I made a claim that the conscious mind was not big enough and would be in disarray if it had to store and disseminate all the affairs of life. Whelan's statement regarding "chaos" vindicates my claim. Also mentioned in the article was journalist Malcolm Gladwell's treatment of *Blink: The Power of Thinking Without Thinking*, which remained on the bestseller lists for four weeks. Also quoted is Clinton Kilts, a professor in the Department of Psychiatry and Behavioral Sciences at Emory University. "There is nothing that you do, there is no thought that you have, there is no awareness, there is no lack of awareness, there is nothing that marks your daily existence that doesn't have a neuro code ..." To paraphrase, it takes a giant warehouse to store all this stuff and everything is marked, labeled, and categorized in our subconscious. This overwhelmingly supports our subconscious mind as the cause of our behavior. Can anything more be said or more accurately stated in summarizing the subconscious neural causes that control our behavior? This proves that most of what goes on in our mind takes place in the subconscious. This casts a new light on our first impressions and snap judgements, which may not be as "snap" or "first" as thought due to the lightning speed of the synapses and neural pathways. This is said in reference to Gladwell's *Blink*. As a journalist and educator, I claim that the subconscious mind is a powerful force and is The First Great Educator and deserving of the teacher award of all time, second only to The Holy Spirit and more powerful than the largest computer. If you think this is an exaggeration, think of what you automatically do before you have time to think of it consciously. Recall what we were told in the conscious and subconscious experiments. The subconscious mind knows what we are going to do before we consciously know it. This stuff is voodoo and insulting to a FWer but the Bible tells us the Holy Spirit empowers the Christian to think in a Godly manner both consciously and unconsciously. Romans 7:25 states: "Thanks be to God through Jesus Christ our Lord! So then on the one hand I myself with my <u>mind</u> am serving the law of God, but on the other, with my flesh the law of sin." The only way "flesh" can be translated here is it refers to his sin nature. Romans 8:23 states"…waiting eagerly for our adoption as sons, the redemption of our body." Body or flesh symbolically represents our sin nature and is the last thing to be redeemed, the first being soul and spirit. Paul is saying his sinful flesh is pulling him one way and his mind, the other way. This implies the Bible teaches the existence of conscious and subconscious minds. Paul uses the word "mind" in a singular sense but the context is unmistakably plural. He is saying his sinful flesh is pulling him … Paul is saying he is doing two things and implies doing them at once. Science is proving that our subconscious mind has a split-second jump on our conscious awareness. Proof of our divided mind has been known for many years scientifically but no one has pointed out that there is proof of the dualistic and divided aspects that can be found in the Bible. I ran across this by accident and I believe Paul substantiates this. This biblical proof that our mind is composed of conscious and subconscious elements is found in several parts of the Bible. Paul is saying he is consciously aware of his sin because it can be seen, represented by his body, and therefore recognizing our conscious brain. Romans 7:17 states: "So now, no longer am I the one doing it, but sin which indwells in me." This indwelling of sin has implications of the innate aspects of genetic transfer of sin from Adam to us. Sin is ingrained in us. It is a powerful and profound truth that Adam's sin was transferred to all humankind and this is recognized in the Christian world but what is not fully recognized is how this transference occurred. When Adam sinned, most Christians agree that he died spiritually but they may not agree that this transference of sin was a genetic process. Elsewhere in this Book, I acknowledged that I am not infallible but I claim that when he died, sin attacked the genetic structure of his physical body and subsequently ours, meaning that sin is so pervasive that it can destroy both spirit and body and this is easily proven by the Bible. The only way it can destroy our body from one generation to the next is through genetic inheritance. I have not found any commentaries that substantiate my claim but the following verses do even though the word "gene" is not used. Proverbs 8:36 states "But he who sins against Me (caps mine) injures himself…" Romans 5:12 tells us "Therefore, just as through one man, sin entered the world, and death through sin, and in this way death came…." Romans 6:23 states "For the wages of sin is death…." Romans 7:5 states "For while we were in the flesh, the sinful passions, which were aroused by the Law, were at work in the members of our body to bear fruit for death." The above Romans 7:17 establishes the cause and effect dual role function of the mind. Paul is not a sinner although he sins. Throughout these passages, Paul allows no room for FW. It's clear he is being influenced by sin nature causes he cannot control. He doesn't want to sin but something compels him to do what he doesn't want to do, thus showing his Dr. Jeckle and Mr. Hyde dual personality syndrome. Our sinful nature is manifested in both our conscious and subconscious minds. Verse 16 states "But if I do the very thing I do not wish to do…." Science proves that we are prompted by our subconscious minds which proves that we both knowingly and subconsciously sin. This can be proven scientifically when a Christian tells a lie automatically, so to speak, and don't realize it until the Holy Spirit gives him a nudge. This was made popular in Freud's day when he discovered that a person will automatically tell the truth, through a subconscious reflex, and then modify it by lying because the truth creates a problem. This establishes the biblical basis of the unconscious mind while proving the falseness of FW. If Paul only had one mind, there would not be a conflict. In order for conflict to be present, it requires a protagonist and antagonist. The Holy Spirit is in conflict with our sin nature and this explains the Bible teaching that our war is waged in the battlefield of the mind. In Paul's case, he committed a sin, a sin he did not want to do. He then says it was not him that did it but the Devil made him do it, i.e., his sin nature.

Paul was referring to the nature of sin, which we can't avoid no matter how we try. An analogy between not wanting to sin and a robbery can be made. If I hold a gun to your head and demand your money, you are going to want to give it to me if you want to live but at the same time, you do not want to give me your money. You are going to want to but don't want to. This is not an oxymoron. If you want to die, you will not want to give me your money. If you want to live, you will both not want to give me your money but want to. When you do something that you consciously did not intend to do, (there is a difference between "intend" and "want") there is only one way to describe this. It really may have been the Devil that did it even if you are a Christian. It could have been the Holy Spirit. Regardless of what the cause was, it was done through the subconscious mind. In Paul's case, he is rhetorically admitting he committed a sin, a sin he did not want to do. In essence then, he is saying that his commission of a sin was done subconsciously. I did not know until I started this book how explicit the Bible is on our subconscious and conscious minds. The fact is you don't do something consciously unless you want to do it, even if you are forced to do it. Stated another way, you may not want to do something, but if you do it, you want to do something you didn't want to do. This is the paradox Paul was describing. Sometimes we sin deliberately consciously. Since our subconscious mind is a repository of the conscious mind, sometimes we sin unconsciously. This explains how our sin nature permeates mind, body, and spirit.

We are aware of some of the things we do but can't be aware of why we do most things. The caveat is we are only aware of five percent of everything we do. In Marianne Szegedy Maszak's article, she stated "According to cognitive neuroscientists, we are conscious of only 5 percent of our cognitive activity, so most of our decisions, actions, emotions, and behavior depends on the 95 percent of brain activity that goes beyond our conscious awareness. From the beating of our hearts to the pushing of the grocery cart and not smashing into the kitty litter, we rely on something that is called the adaptive unconscious, which is all the ways that our brains understand the world that the mind and body must negotiate. The adaptive unconscious makes it possible for us to turn a corner in our car without having to go through elaborate calculations to determine the precise angle of the turn, the velocity of the automobile, the steering radius of the car". This brings to mind what I have heard all my life, that we use only 5 percent of our brain. This misguided axiom, or poor choice of words, wrongly conveys that the other 95 percent lays dormant and unused and carries the erroneous idea that the other 95 percent was wasted or unused. There are four key points to the article: (1) Of the tens of thousands of things we do daily, we are only aware of five percent *as we are doing them.* Another point that was made was of this five percent that we are aware of, we don't know the primary cause. After a period of time, this five percent is reduced further. Limiting our conscious memory capacity to only 5 percent of the events and things that happen is in drastic disagreement to what Plato seems to have said in "Theaetetus" unless he was referring to the subconscious memory. He compared memory to a wax tablet which would capture whatever was pressed on it. He called memory the scribe of the soul. However, he would be in line with modern science if he viewed the mind as composed of conscious and separate subconscious sections. It should be noted that some scientists do not agree with the 95 to 5 ratios but for those who do, if we do ten thousand things, (my estimate) we are consciously aware of five hundred. We easily do ten-thousand things daily, counting opening our car door, turning the ignition, viewing hundreds of things on the highway on the way home, etc. This is in reference to everything we do, scratching our head, waving to the neighbor, seeing a dog on the road, etc. In making a list and recalling those five hundred, we would only remember (without help) maybe two or three dozen. But the most important number is where did those other nine thousand and five hundred things that happened to you go, things that you were not aware of? They were neuronally coded along with the other five hundred things and stored in the vast library of the subconscious mind. This is agreeing with the Bible that tells us we will be accountable for all things and this implies that our subconscious memory will be opened as witness against us. Since we are only consciously aware of five percent of everything that happens to us (including thoughts, smells, etc.), we should think of the subconscious mind as a large sponge holding a vast library of information and the conscious mind holding one page or one book. Every event or thought has its own neural code. We non-scientists cannot grasp the scope of this even though we know our brain has millions of neurons. One of the questions I have is since a neuron is responsible for recording a thought, what happens to the thoughts that were stored in the brain cells that die as we age? It's impossible to comprehend the trillion things that have been recorded in the subconscious. I am suspicious of this capacity. Doesn't it ever get full? Don't some of it just fade away? Part of my answer is in the documentaries that show a person under hypnosis can remember things that happened fifty or more years ago. (2) Science has coined a new phrase, adaptive unconscious (AU). This describes what our brain must do to understand what our mind and body must automatically do to get us through our twenty- four hour day. It allows us to step up a stairway without thinking. The tens of thousands of things we do daily are done subconsciously. This explains the weakening of our minds as we get older when we forget to leave the keys on the hook. In essence, our subconscious mind is controlling our conscious mind. AU is necessary because our conscious mind is not big enough to orchestrate all the movements and thoughts necessary for us to consciously conduct the affairs of daily living. This is hard science to digest for those who feel they are in control. Dissecting the word "control" is key to understanding the difference between will and FW. God wants us to feel secure. It's been proven that insecurity causes stress and stress causes an elevation in cortisol and too much cortisol causes disease. God does not want us to think we are the cause of our control but He wants us to feel some degree of control. As an example, He wants us to come to Him willingly even though His grace has a magnetic pull which is biblically proven whose force we can't resist. What's difficult to understand about our mind is we can consciously watch this control process at work in imagining technology which allows a technician to see what's happening a fraction of a second before the subject knows it will happen. AU allows us to step up a stairway without thinking. It's alarming to realize that of the tens of thousands of things we do daily, they are done subconsciously. It's hard to believe that John Calvin taught this in an indirect way, and without the use of the scientific method, five hundred years ago and without any medical knowledge. At that time not much was known about mind/brain functions. He did this by teaching against FW and for bondage; he was in effect teaching that our will was controlled by something outside self. His father wanted him to be a Catholic priest but he changed his goal to be a lawyer and used his legal acumen to dissect the Bible. This is why FW theologians fight Calvinism to the death. The terms robot and determinism are two favorite words used frequently to undermine Calvinism. I have read many books and articles that claim that someone who thinks he has been chosen by God (a Calvinist) is not a Christian and instead is a puppet who allows his strings to be pulled by mysterious forces that are contrived for self-fulfilling purposes. Actually, this claim is partially true. We are robots in a sense but Calvinistic literature avoids this comparison. The comparison to a robot is correct in that if you are chosen by God, you are predetermined and set in motion. It does not mean that everything we do is predetermined by God. Sin is predetermined in the sense that God turned the earth over to the prince of the power of the air, as stated in Ephesians 2:2. Going back to the Garden, sin has reigned since the Adamic Fall. It does not necessarily mean that Calvinists think that we are programmed to go to the store, make a trip, or read a book and it does not mean that we don't jump God's predetermined fence and sometimes stray. (3) Researchers have found that smell plays a strong unconscious role in our mating choices and is the strongest of our senses. The female sense of smell is stronger than that of the male. I have finally found out after all these years why I was attracted to my wife. I loved her but there was something else going on. Smell is a strong motivator that has a strong influence on other situations in addition to mating. It's a strong role because our brains were designed (Darwin would say evolved) to give preference and precedence to olfactory perception. As a side note, I believe that when Adam lost his dominion over his animals and they no longer saw him as their ruler, he needed a strong survival weapon (sense of smell) in addition to his eyes that serves well in close quarters or heavy brush. I believe that the pre-Fall Garden was a preview of Heaven. I don't believe my side note is conjecture because Adam had no need to kill animals.

God created Adam with all the senses he needed, fully developed and suited for the environment he was in. Genesis 1:26 tells us "...and let them rule ..." which shows Adam's rule over his kingdom. Genesis 2:19 tells us "...and brought them to the man to see what he would call them ... ." This suggests that the beasts were domesticated to the point that Adam could rule them. This was possible in the absence of sin. This parallels a future time when the lion will lay with the lamp because of the absence of sin. Domestication of the animals is proven in Genesis 1:28, " ...and fill the earth and subdue it ... ." Adam had no weapons yet God told him to rule and subdue the animals and earth. The only way Adam could carry out God's instructions was for Adam to have control of his animals to a point that is not possible today. But after the Fall and the harshness of life on the outside, his anatomy changed to compensate. Science has proven that when our bodies undergo changes such as loss of sight, our hearing perception increases. Over time and colder climates, his body hair probably became coarser. The climate in the pre-Fall Garden was temperate and scripture tells us he had no need for protective clothing. We know the only suitable clothing for early man was animal skin and fur. In regards to our present-day sense of smell, couples are subconsciously drawn together because of it. Even in the face of the hard facts of science, I suspect FWers will argue that they chose their mates independent of any outside influences and apart from factors except their FW initiative. Their argument for FW is standard rejection based on their ability to consciously reject impulses such as smell. It's true that smell can be ignored but this does not make a case for FW. The validity of FW cannot be based on the ability to say yes or no. Its validity is based entirely on cause and effect. If the woman says yes to a smell and creates a relationship, that relationship was caused by smell, not FW. If she says no to the smell, that no was caused by a force stronger than the force of smell, like maybe the man was unattractive. In either case, FW played no part. In getting back to the unconscious attraction created by smell, when a person loses some or all of his hearing, his sense of balance deteriorates. Our brain is designed to give preference and precedence to olfactory perception. Did Adam have this perception originally or did it develop over time? In modern times, couples are subconsciously drawn together because of smell. In ancient times, our senses were primarily for survival. If you want your marriage to survive, give your wife a heartfelt compliment, give her a sniff, look her in the eye, and say "Honey, I have loved you from the first day I smelled you." Our sense of smell, although not as acute, places us alongside the lower animal world. (4) The nose plays more of a role than just for finding mates. When two females room together, it's been show that many times their menstrual cycle synchronizes because the "unconscious perception" of odor sets off their endocrine system. According to the above U. S. News and World Report article, this means that some odors by pass the normal loop that first goes to our genes that carry smell to our conscious senses and instead takes a direct path to our unconscious senses. Was this by-passing function developed in ancient man to increase his survivability or was Adam and Eve created with it? The odors that don't reach our conscious senses nevertheless have a significant influence on our behavior and it's a tossup as to which is the most influential, odors that are recognized and those that are not. Obviously, FW has no hand in behavior caused by smell. As stated above, the sense of smell is the most powerful of our senses. Research has also shown that many people with schizophrenia suffer from olfactory impairment which is in conjunction with dysfunction in their higher brain centers which are responsible for understanding and recognizing social cues. Smell is the window that reveals sociability disorders that reside in the subconscious mind.

CONCLUSION

This book highlights the attack on FW but in the name of balance, it must be noted that FW is not yet dead according to those scientists who think that it is too early for a funeral. Instead, FW is due for more check-ups and doctor appointments. This is because science never announces the conclusive end to anything because the scientific method dictates continual research. Just because a scientific theory has been researched and developed past the hypothesis stage does not necessarily mean it's ready to be classified as fact. The problem is there are just as many versions of the scientific method as there are scientists. The issue of the mind/brain is such that it is not now, or may never be, fully understood. I base my claim on the simple scriptural depictions that state that God made man in His image and God's statement in describing Himself as the "I Am". Being the image of God is not a simple matter. Like Him, we are not easy to define. Even after gene mapping, scientists are still debating what constitutes the mind and the dichotomy of the mind/brain relationship. In telling us who He is, there is no language that can impart His dimensions. The mind and brain are like outer space. We may never know how large it is. One favorable review of FW research stated that if physical laws are "deterministic", then there is no such thing as FW. If physical laws contain "probabilistic" elements or "quantum indeterminacy", FW does not exist. This kind of exploration is over my head or at least beyond my interest because I am unable to determine if the issue is how to determine if something is indeterminant. Throughout this book, I have based my opinions on the simplicity of cause and effect but I find out that cause and effect is not so simple when put under the microscope of "indeterminacy". Another review mentions "modular epiphenomenalism" as a possible factor when discussing the nature of FW. It goes on to discuss the hypothesis that our conscious will may play a crucial role in planning and forming intentions, therefore making FW plausible. When googling FW, there are scores of pro FW articles, enough for me to acknowledge that FW is here to stay and the hard evidence against FW in some scientific communities will continue to be ignored the same way it is ignored in the religious and secular communities.

The above mention of determinism brings to mind one idea that some scientists have about determinism and its relationship with cause and effect. This idea holds that all events in the world are the result of some previous event. I can relate to this because I believe in cause and effect without equivocation. Unlike FW that has many faces, cause and effect is constant and unchanging. If everything has been predetermined and nothing new can exist under the sun, I wonder if this is what Solomon meant when he said there is nothing new. In corelating this with genetic inheritance, the continuum factor cannot be disputed and this anti-FW evidence can't be ignored. My behavior is the result of my genetic makeup and environmental factors. In discussing determinism versus FW, behavioral social scientists have joined the fray by pointing out the dangers of teaching determinism and the moral implications resulting from believing that FW does not exist. We would have no reason to take responsibility for our actions. Our inclination to do good would lessen. Our moral good would be polluted, and so on. But these concerns should be dismissed by the Christian world. Science has several definitions of determinism but the most popular one is that it is controlled by the law of physics which, as stated above, determines all events in this world and the universe. This parallels the religious definition and is called predestation, which is caused by God's law. I believe that the law of God and the law of physics is the same because He created physics. The word "predestation" is not used by science because predestation does not fit under a microscope. The closest it came was when gene mapping discovered the so-called God gene. A person was connected to a monitor and asked to think about God or another higher source, as in transcendental meditation. A specific section of his brain lit up. Experimentation showed that these genes were exclusively used for that purpose and humans were the only ones who had them. Determinism is characterized in some circles as being fatalistic, meaning that we have no recourse. If something bad has been set in motion and can't be stopped, it will cause a person to be negative, pessimistic, depressed, and powerless to do anything about it. But fatalism leaves God out of the picture. With Him in, even if a tornado is on the horizon, a Christian will become frightened but will not be without hope. God told us there will be wars and rumors of wars but He did not leave us without hope. Fatalism is the law of science and physics without God. Sovereignty and predestination is the law of God.

William James said in Principles of Psychology "Nature in her unfathomable designs has mixed us of clay and flame, of brain and mind, that the two things hang indubitably together and determine each other's being, but how or why, no mortal may ever know." With these words, he has set an inexorable backdrop in the mysteries of the mind/brain complex. Somewhere in these dempsey dumpster containers, what gene markers and neuroscientists classify as our conscious and subconscious minds, are neural codes representing every joy, sorrow, image, hope, fear, and aspiration that is a composite representation of our lives. This is what this book has attempted to capture in a few pages in proving the foolishness of FW.

Clinton Kilts (page 80) said everything we do or think has a neural code. The brains neocortex is the largest of the brain's two part segment and contains 100 billion cells. Within these billions of cells are where the neural codes reside. Most of our behavior is shaped by our subconscious minds. Within this vast realm, there is a 24/7 video recorder (even while we sleep) that does not appear to have a delete button. One way we know this is research in hypnosis. Another proof is gene mapping. Our recorder can sometimes malfunction. What we perceive to see and what we actually see may not be the same. However, a phenomenal testimony of Kilt's research is my personal experience when I was maybe one and a half years old. I was not old enough to crawl and I remember feeling trapped lying on my back on a quilt under a tree in a field filled with what looked like white snow balls. I can still remember 78 years later the smell of urine on a multi-colored quilt. This also reinforces other research in this book that tells us our sense of smell is more acute than our other senses.

Descartes (page 27) a FW believer, may be partially right when he said "I think. Therefore I am." He though that one segment of the brain was where FW resides and was also where the soul lived. In this he was proven right. (discovery of the God gene) He was also right if he intended the "I am" to mean it represented our history, which is reflected in the history of our subconscious mind. It will be this history, including junk mail, that will be opened and judged by Jesus when we hope to hear these words, "Well done, good and faithful slave... ." (Matthew 25:23) The mind is a terrible thing to waste and after having re-read the scripture pertaining to my subconscious mind, I have renewed my efforts to be a faithful slave and have become strengthened in my efforts to focus on Christ's will, not FW. Thanks to Kilts and other neuroscientists, this book has been able to corelate science, the Bible, and the fallacy of FW.

SCRIPTURE

Used to affirm predestination

Matt. 22:14/ Matt. 11: 25-27/John 15:16/Romans 8:28-30 and 9:10-24/ Eph 1:4 and 2:10/Rev. 13:8/1 Thess. 1:4-5

Used to deny predestination

John 3:16/Matt. 18:11 and 1:21/2Peter 3:9/Romans 8:32-34/Hebrews 9:15

As far as salvation is concerned, it makes no difference what we believe regarding predestination. If you have been chosen, you are secure. FWers believe God has chosen all but some have failed to chose Him. In effect, they believe God allows FW to override His will.

Used to affirm Calvinism, bondage, other non-free will verses

Luke 19:41-44/Luke 22:22/Romans 9:14-21/2Th 2:11-12/John 2:24/John 12:40/Romans 9:17-18

Romans 11:7-10/Phil 2:13/Mark 4:11/Mark 6:52/Mark 8:17/Luke 8:10/ Luke 9:45/Luke 18:34/Luke 19:41-44/Luke 24:16/Matt 11:25-27/Luke 10:21/Romans 9:11/1Col 1:26-30/Eph 1:4,5,11/1Tim 12:14/2Tim 1:9/1Tim 3:9/Luke 11:49-50/John 9:1-3/John 12:27/Romans 9:22-23/Gal 3:22/

John 6:24/John 8:43-47/Romans 3:9-18and23/Romans 8:5-17/1/1Col 2:10,12,14/2Col4:3-4/Eph 5:17-19

Used to affirm free will

Matt 11:28/Luke 9:23/Luke 11:9/John 1:12/John 3:36/John 6:40/John 7:17/John 10:9/John 12:26/John 16:27/1Peter 1:1-2/John 7:17/John 1:7-9/ John 12-32/Matt 18:14/1Tim 2:3/2Peter 3:9/John 1:7-9/John 12:32/1Corin 15:22/2Corin 5:14-15/2Corin 5:19/1Tim 2:6/1Tim 4:9-10/Tim 2:11/Acts 7:51/2Corin 6:1

All above does not constitute a comprehensive list; my intent was to list some of the most used.

In refuting the claims of free will, I am taking one scripture, the flagship of free will theology, and attempting to make it representative of some of the other scripture whose interpretation is questionable. *John 3:16:*

For God so loved the world that He gave his only begotten Son, that whosoever believeith in Him should not perish, but have everlasting life. The word world is used 222 times in the Bible and not once does it refer to every individual in the world without exception. There are many individual people that He hates. In Psalm 5:5, He hates workers of iniquity. The word world is a generic term defining God as a God of love for His creation. Another misinterpretation is the word whosoever. This does not mean anyone can believe. Scripture proves that some are unable to believe. Regardless of claims of free will, some are only free to serve Satan. If their freedom is thus curtailed, how can they be free to believe? The core of this phrase promises that those who can believe will not perish. This does not promise salvation to all. Another example of misinterpretation is *11 Peter 3:9.......* not wishing for any to perish but for all to come to repentance. The core belief of free will is that God wants no one to perish and all to be saved despite the fact that it was God that "made the path narrow to salvation and wide to destruction" and dozens of times, causes dozens of people to be hardened and thus unable to believe. Calvinists who are knowledgeable in exegesis claim that this verse is referring to God's elect and it was them who Peter was referring to. If this is correct, the purpose of this verse was to make the core belief emphasis the long suffering of God.

"There is nothing when movement is absent"
A. EINSTEIN (WHICH IS ANOTHER WAY OF SAYING THAT SOMETHING HAS TO CAUSE MOVEMENT)

Printed in the United States
By Bookmasters